A Home for Our Heritage

When we are through, we shall have reproduced American life as lived; and that, I think, is the best way of preserving at least a part of our history and tradition. For by looking at things that people used and that show the way they lived, a better and truer impression can be gained than could be had in a month of reading—even if there were books whose authors had the facilities to discover the minute details of the older life.

—HENRY FORD

A Home for Our Heritage

The Building and Growth of Greenfield Village and Henry Ford Museum, 1929-1979

by Geoffrey C. Upward
MUSEUM EDITOR

The Henry Ford Museum Press
Dearborn, Michigan

To Mr. Ford, who left such an incredible story for us to tell

A publication of
The Henry Ford Museum Press,
The Edison Institute, Dearborn, Michigan   48121

Library of Congress Cataloging in Publication Data

Upward, Geoffrey C   1950-
  A home for our heritage.

  Includes index.
  1. Edison Institute (Henry Ford Museum and
Greenfield Village) Dearborn, Mich. — History.
2. Ford, Henry, 1863-1947. I. Title.
E161.U68   977.4'33   79-19068
ISBN 0-933728-30-1
ISBN 0-933728-29-8 pbk.

Designed by Don Ross, Don Ross Associates, Detroit, Michigan
Typeset by The McKay Press, Midland, Michigan
Printed and bound by Thomson-Shore, Dexter, Michigan

Contents

An Appreciation

Henry Ford the Collector

by Wendell Garrett
Editor and Publisher, The Magazine Antiques

The concept of history as exhibits and objects, rather than schoolbooks and words, seems to have dawned upon Henry Ford suddenly. Here was a new type of collection and a new kind of collector, somewhat unique and prophetic. In assembling an enormous collection of infinite variety he aimed to form a great museum-school of life. This thoughtfully conceived educational project reflected his deep attachment to the sights and sounds of rural life and his enduring affinity for the traditional past of agrarian America and its virtues of self-reliance, hard work and thrift. His social outlook of rugged individualism stemmed in large part from the moral precepts of the McGuffey *Readers* that were the staple of his formal education in the rural schools he attended as a boy.

Halfway between Boston and Worcester on Route 20 in South Sudbury, Massachusetts, stands the "ancient hostelry" called the Red Horse Tavern, known since the publication of Longfellow's 1863 *Tales* as the Wayside Inn. Ford fell in love with the battered old building in 1922 and bought it in June 1923. In time, the Wayside Inn property with its affiliated farms and schools, which Ford's agents assembled for him, spread over 88 parcels of land totaling 2,667 acres in the towns of Sudbury, Framingham and Marlborough. Ford selected the Wayside Inn as a showcase, a working model for the much bigger museum he was planning to build at Dearborn.

The way in which Ford worked out a suitable scheme for attracting and pleasing the American public would eventually affect profoundly the historic preservation movement and the concept of museum villages in the United States. This was the first place where an individual, possessing all of the necessary money, set out to restore and put on display not just one famous building, but a large, functioning community of homes, farms, schools, craft industries, chapel and village tavern — intended, as Ford stated it, "to show how our forefathers lived and to bring to mind what kind of people they were." The results of this experiment were mixed, but through this pilot project he began a new era.

Ford's matured concept of history as the appreciation and study of "the general resourcefulness of our people" lives on in the vast collections and the more than 100 buildings of the Henry Ford Museum-Greenfield Village complex at Dearborn. In assembling the collection, he told his agents, "Get everything you can find! I want at least one of every tool, utensil or machine ever used." This has become by far one of the most educational panoramas of American ideas and products in the United States operated by a foundation and with its own private funding.

Based on Ford's belief that "the farther you look back, the farther you can look ahead," the complex would remind people how far and how fast America had come in technical progress over the past century or two. Ford hoped that once this had been vividly realized there would be greater belief in and more purposeful striving for a similar degree of future progress. His scheme was meant to go much farther than mere visual illustration, for it included a school system, a campus, a laboratory for the people of America that would "emphasize the pioneer qualities of self-dependence and resourcefulness that carved this country out of the wilderness."

With the museum and village binding together the past, present and future, it was Ford's strong conviction that visitors should become familiar through observation with the various mechanical difficulties overcome by their ancestors by learning to carry on the old crafts with old tools under the old conditions carefully simulated. His aim was to teach American history in a vivid way by using antiques and buildings to demonstrate how our ancestors lived and worked. He tried, he said, "to assemble a complete series of every article used or made in America from the days of the first settlers down to the present time."

A thread of "Americanism" in historical sequence holds this enormous collection together. The museum collections therefore contain: a department devoted to the development of agriculture showing all types of farm equipment, from the hand tools and simple, horse-drawn implements of the 18th century to modern tractor-powered machinery; a department devoted to land and air transportation, showing a broad collection of historic and significant horse-drawn vehicles, bicycles, motorcycles, railway locomotives, street cars, fire engines, aircraft, automobiles and trucks; a department devoted to the household arts; and a superb decorative arts collection including furniture, glass, crockery and china, clocks, stoves, lighting devices, pewter, britannia ware, silver, pictures, books, textiles and costumes.

All of these relics have one thing in common: Ford's obsession with the common man, the material culture of the middling sort, not the arts of the elite. The whole display, then, is supremely American in its vastness, its democracy and its reaching into the past that formal history has traditionally ignored.

Foreword

The Edison Institute, founded by Henry Ford to preserve physical reminders of American history, has its own history. *A Home for Our Heritage* offers, for the first time, the comprehensive story of its building and growth. The text and hundreds of previously unpublished photographs are drawn from the institute's tremendous resources, particularly the Ford Archives, which houses millions of documents and artifacts relating to Mr. Ford's personal and business lives.

Henry Ford was always "Mr. Ford" to me and to virtually every person who ever worked for him. My career at the institute began in 1931. Since 1976 it has been my privilege to direct the destinies of his educational vision. Communicating America's great heritage to visitors from all over the world has challenged me and hundreds of other staff members through the years. The challenge is bigger than ever as we mark the institute's 50th anniversary. For, this year we will highlight and interpret not only the country's past, but events from our own history as well.

The beginning of our colorful story predates the village and museum's formal dedication in 1929. As early as 1924, while restoring the Wayside Inn at South Sudbury, Massachusetts, Henry Ford expressed his hope that the American people could "have a look at history as intimate and alive, instead of as something pressed dead within a book." For a time, he definitely considered reconstructing an early New England village on the more than 2,500 acres he had acquired surrounding the historic inn.

One year later his plans had changed. Though he did not publicly announce his project until 1928, he had decided to build a museum and historic village in Dearborn, Michigan. These, he contemplated, would serve as a "living textbook of human and technical history . . . an illustrated course in comparative civilization," stressing the pioneer virtues of independence and hard work that made "self-reliant men and women who could largely fend for themselves in good times and bad."

Mr. Ford had long prepared himself for this undertaking. He started collecting Edisoniana in 1905 with the acquisition of Edison phonographs and experimental phonographic apparatus. He began his collection of McGuffey *Readers* in 1914 and within two decades it numbered 468 copies, representing 145 different editions.

In 1919 he restored his family home on its original site, pioneering in the field of American archaeology to obtain evidence for furnishings. Following this came restorations of the Wayside Inn and the Botsford Tavern, west of Detroit.

Launched in 1920, his collecting program moved swiftly forward to include household artifacts, engines and machines documenting technological advances and historic buildings. Little escaped his scrutiny and consideration. By 1922 his search for and acquisitions of Americana reached large-scale proportions, carried on by antique dealers, Ford representatives, special agents and Mr. Ford himself. Gifts poured in from interested donors across the country. To preserve endangered structures, he purchased the Clinton (Michigan) Inn and the Waterford (Michigan) General Store in 1927, one year before the proposed creation of Greenfield Village became public news.

At the dedication of his museum and village as The Edison Institute in honor of Thomas A. Edison on October 21, 1929, various buildings already stood in the village. These included the complete Menlo Park Compound from New Jersey, the Abraham Lincoln Courthouse from Illinois, Luther Burbank's garden office from California, the Phoenixville Post Office from Connecticut and the Whittier Toll House / Shoe Shop from Massachusetts.

The rapid building pace continued until the early 1940s. Rare was the year that three or more structures were not added to the village. Though major activity ceased by 1944 (probably because of World War II, the death in 1943 of Mr. Ford's only son, Edsel, and Mr. Ford's advancing age) the village has continued to grow. During 1977 and 1978, an early-18th-century Connecticut saltbox house was moved here and re-erected at the end of "residential row." With this latest addition, village buildings numbered more than 100.

The 14-acre museum building, centered around an exact replica of that most American of structures, Independence Hall, contained on completion a fine collection of American decorative arts and an unmatchable collection of mechanical arts.

Fifty years after Ford's initial collecting efforts, refinements and additions have placed the decorative arts among the five finest public collections in the nation. The mechanical arts treasures — transportation, communications, lighting, shop machinery, power, agriculture and home arts — remain unsurpassed.

However one views Greenfield Village and Henry Ford Museum, one must always appreciate Henry Ford's role in their formation. He was a collector with vision, a man who established collecting patterns for others. His efforts in the field of Americana predate those of the Rockefellers, the duPonts, the Garvans. He recovered those common, everyday artifacts that no one else considered or would consider. His work in archaeology and the conservation of artifacts launched the exacting sciences we know today. He made mistakes, of course, for he traveled an uncharted course. But he led the way for others to follow. As Mr. Ford once commented in a *New York Times* interview: "There was no way for me to escape doing what I did. I had an idea, and it was impossible to get away from it; it just had to be born." Although his remarks concerned the quadricycle, he undoubtedly felt the same about the birth and development of his second love — The Edison Institute.

The village and museum today are beginning to take their rightful place on the national scene. Major development programs supported the complete redesign of the mechanical arts exhibits, the creation of a conservation laboratory and increased visitor amenities. A revitalized and expanding education program now covers grammar schools, high schools, colleges and universities, as well as adult education, museum internships and teacher training in the use of museum resources. While phase one of the development program concluded with the opening of the new eight-acre Hall of Technology in the summer of 1979, phase two is in the planning stage.

Any museum that does not move forward must stagnate and eventually die. This will not happen to Greenfield Village and Henry Ford Museum. Fifty years from now, in A.D. 2029, this institution will be more active than ever in documenting for American and foreign visitors the story of America's past and its progress to the present.

FRANK CADDY
President, The Edison Institute

1914-1926

*When you once get an idea in which you
believe with all your heart, work it out. Do
not take it to others for their opinions
about it, for if you do, before you know it,
that idea will be all cumbered up with other
people's modifications and changes and
additions, and it will no longer be your idea.
Go ahead and work it out the way it
came to you.*

—HENRY FORD

Chapter One

Learning by Doing

One summer day about three years ago, in that part of Michigan which forms the great thumb along the shore of Lake Huron, an automobile was seen to stop suddenly. Then it was backed over the road for several hundred feet. Out of the car stept [sic] a man who hurried to something which looked like a long-discarded stove buried in the sand. But little of it was visible, merely the rounded side being exposed to indicate what it might be. The man summoned his companion, and the two worked for more than an hour to remove it. Under the hot sun they dug and scraped away until at last the thing they sought was exposed to view. The elder man looked it over carefully, shook his head a little sadly, spoke to his companion, and the two of them climbed into the car and drove away.

The man was Henry Ford; his companion, his son Edsel.

Literary Digest, *July 14, 1923*

Henry Ford, the fledgling collector, worked up a sweat that summer day in 1920, fervently pursuing a goal to re-create the physical surroundings of his boyhood. The object of that particular search was an 1867 "Starlight" Model 25 stove, made by the Detroit Stove Works. Such a stove had heated the parlor of the Dearborn, Michigan, farmhouse where he grew up in the decade following the Civil War. Now a millionaire industrialist, Ford was in the process of restoring the house with what most would consider extreme standards of accuracy.

A year and a half later, after initiating a nationwide search by stove companies and Ford car dealers, he found the prize rusting on a Stockbridge, Massachusetts, porch. Dismantling the $25 acquisition himself, he loaded it in his trunk for the journey back to his boyhood home. Little did Ford know that in a matter of years he would be preserving and furnishing a home of far greater magnitude than the simple, white-frame farmhouse of his youth — a home for the most treasured artifacts of the nation's heritage.

The inspiration behind Henry Ford's desire to create Greenfield Village and Henry Ford Museum is hard to trace; even Ford was unsure of the origins. A few seemingly unrelated projects undertaken between 1914 and 1926, however, shed some light on his growing interest in creating what later would be called a living textbook of Americana.

Although Henry Ford had developed from a farm boy with a mechanical bent into one of the world's most powerful and wealthy industrialists, he and his wife, Clara, never forgot the values of the rural life they had left behind. Collecting tangible evidence of that earlier existence became a passion, especially for Henry. The clocks and watches he had loved tinkering with and repairing since childhood days had grown into a collection. Shortly after the turn of the century, Ford began accumulating items associated with his lifelong hero, Thomas Edison. He started storing a few miscellaneous items picked up through the years in a spare office at the Ford Motor Company's Highland Park plant as early as 1906-07. In 1914, however, a nearly insignificant incident spurred his first truly ambitious search for artifacts.

His wife of 26 years, Clara, watching some children playing on their way home from school one afternoon, suddenly blurted out: "Hear the children gaily shout/'Half past four and school is out!'" Both Fords mistakenly thought the verse came from the first of William Holmes McGuffey's *Eclectic Readers* (published between 1836 and 1920), but neither could recall the rest of the rhyme. After fruitlessly searching the house for a copy of the *Reader*, Henry decided to inquire among friends and, if necessary, bookstores to see if they had one. By the late 1930s, he had collected some 468 copies of 145 different editions, amassing one of the world's three best collections.

Throughout his life Henry Ford often quoted the simple, fundamental philosophies of McGuffey, from whose *Readers* both he and his wife had been educated. The one-room school concept and McGuffey himself would figure prominently in the future Greenfield Village.

Shortly after Clara's utterance, however, Ford became involved with a much more serious problem related to his views on the past and its usefulness to a modern world. In 1916, after publishing a series of three articles based on interviews with the auto magnate (who then was vocally supporting United States pacifism in World War I), the *Chicago Tribune* (which stood for United States preparedness) ran an editorial calling Ford "an anarchist" and "an ignorant idealist." Ford sued for $1 million with the case coming to trial in Mt. Clemens, Michigan, in 1919.

One of the original articles quoted Ford as saying, "history is more or less bunk." The defense attorneys, trying to prove Ford's "ignorance," quizzed him on this statement and hundreds of others during his eight days on the witness stand. At one point in the pressure-filled repartee with the *Tribune*'s legal counsel, Ford responded to the question, "But history was bunk, and art was no good . . . that was your attitude in 1916?" with, "I did not say it was bunk. It was bunk to me, but I did not say . . . ."

While headlines in the nation's press played up Ford's seeming lack of depth, what he meant then, and explained many times in later years, was that most *written* history reflected little of people's day-to-day existence. "History as it is taught in the schools deals largely with the unusual phases of our national life — wars, major political controversies, territorial extensions and the like," he would say in 1932.

> When I went to our American history books to learn how our forefathers harrowed the land, I discovered that the historians knew nothing about harrows. Yet our country has depended more on harrows than on guns or speeches. I thought that a history which excluded harrows and all the rest of daily life is bunk and I think so yet.

If nothing else, the *Tribune* trial (which Ford won with six cents awarded in damages) made the 56-year-old industrialist collect his thoughts on where his auto-crazy generation had come from and where it was going. He soon began collecting more than thoughts. As he told his secretary, Ernest G. Liebold, on the way home from the trial:

> We're going to start something. I'm going to start up a museum and give people a true picture of the development of the country. That's the only history that is worth observing, that you can preserve in itself. We're going to build a museum that's going to show industrial history, and it won't be bunk! We'll show the people what actually existed in years gone by and we'll show the actual development of American industry from the early days, from the earliest days that we can recollect up to the present day.

That same year, 1919, the existence of Ford's birthplace was jeopardized by the extension of a major road through the family farm. The house lay directly in the proposed highway's path and either had to be demolished or moved. Ford and a few of his relatives decided not only to move the house and barns, but to restore them as well. While furnishing the house, Henry caught the collecting bug full force. The search for the "Starlight #25," for example, unearthed many early stoves. He and his aides scoured farms and antique shops and soon were accumulating enough everyday artifacts for several restorations.

Ford stored excess items in his tractor plant office, located on Oakwood Boulevard in Dearborn. To compound the clutter, the public flooded Ford with offers of antiques when word of his search circulated. By 1920-21, when the company transferred tractor operations to the huge River Rouge manufacturing facility a few miles away, Ford's office was nearly full. Thus, as the tractors moved out, the antiques moved in, occupying part of Building 13. Old objects, from plows to player pianos to traction steam engines, took their places in the bays. Smaller items — inkwells, grease lamps, hunting rifles — were stacked on long tables or benches or hung from the wooden rafters.

As Ford stepped up the pace of his collection and preservation projects, the bays of Building 13 filled accordingly. By 1923 Ford was the primary collector of Americana in the world. Tens of thousands of letters — many of which were answered — poured in yearly from people wanting to give or sell antiques to him. The collections resulting from these offers and Ford's own searches were, in a word, incredible. Henry Ford collected unbelievable quantities of Americana. He collected technological and decorative masterpieces. He collected items associated with names illustrious in America's past. He collected the not-so-great and he collected humbler or everyday objects. The totality alone of his collecting is significant, for if Ford had not preserved these artifacts then, they would not exist today. Other museums have the great things, but it is the lesser items that add depth and meaning to the story of America's development.

"It is not as yet an ordered collection," Ford said in 1926. "We want to have something of everything . . . . One of these days the collection will have its own museum at Dearborn, and there we shall reproduce the life of the country in its every age."

Before committing the Dearborn museum to the drawing board, however, the man initially interested in saving his boyhood home expanded his preservation efforts, both in scope and in geography. In 1923, a number of eastern antiquarians were soliciting funds to save the 1686 Wayside Inn in South Sudbury, Massachusetts. Henry Wadsworth Longfellow immortalized the inn and its Red Horse Tavern in his 1863 collection of poems, *Tales of a Wayside Inn*. But immortal or not, the inn had fallen into disrepair since the death in 1919 of its sympathetic owner

1914-1926

and restorer, Edward R. Lemon. Concerned Bostonians feared the property would fall into uncaring private hands.

The group interested Henry and Clara Ford in the project, but to a greater extent than expected. Ford bought the inn himself and began to acquire what would total 2,600 acres of surrounding land, complete with numerous buildings, in order to preserve the inn's setting.

Ford's chance to show the public his ideas of participatory history led to development of the entire property. Located near the historic jewel itself (which he soon opened to the public) were early schools, a church, craft industries and, of course, farms and homes. To furnish his early American community, Ford sent aides, automobile dealers and antique dealers into the New England countryside. The excess soon crammed the bays of the old tractor plant back in Dearborn.

This functioning, restored Massachusetts village was a first in the United States. Ford did not learn his methods from books or, in this case, even previous experience. He actively participated in turning his envisioned goal into reality and learned in the process.

Despite his incredible wealth, Henry Ford kept a personal hand in the details of the Ford Motor Company's operation. His other interests shared the same personal attention. Whenever they got the chance, Henry and Clara traveled to the Wayside Inn where they could experience quiet times amid the pleasant surroundings or join invited friends in old-fashioned dances. Still, reaching Massachusetts from Dearborn required a good number of hours, especially with the slower travel modes available in the early 1920s. A project closer to home would allow Ford greater involvement.

Whatever his intentions, in 1924 he purchased the 1836 Botsford Tavern, a few miles west of Detroit. For this preservation project he acquired only 41 surrounding acres. After an extensive restoration, during which he was frequently on site, the building served as an informal museum until 1934 when it opened for public dining.

Even closer to home, Ford in 1923 bought and restored the little red schoolhouse he had attended in Dearborn Township's Scotch Settlement district. He operated it for several years as an experimental school where three- to six-year-olds learned from both new visual teaching techniques and McGuffey's first *Reader.*

People could learn much from history, Ford believed. He did not preserve for sentimental reasons, but, as he put it, to demonstrate first to himself and then to his countrymen that "mankind passes from the old to the new on a human bridge formed by those who labor in the three principal arts — agriculture, manufacture, transportation." The vehicle through which Ford would express these ideas — his museum complex at Dearborn — was not far off.

Somehow it seems appropriate that Ford accomplished these preservation projects simply by plunging in and doing them. Part of the reason for his methods may have been that such projects were rare early in the 20th century. Ford is noted, in fact, for breaking ground in historic preservation, restoration, archaeology and collecting. Americans still sought European antiques during the 1920s. Ford's zeal for Americana spurred this country's interest in its own artifacts. Even if a wealth of knowledge on the subject had existed, however, formal education and book learning were just not his style. In his collecting and preservation pursuits, he truly practiced his hard and fast philosophy of education: "learning by doing."

1914-1926

1   2   3

William Ford (1) and his wife Mary Litogot Ford (2) were operating a healthy farm when Henry was born on July 30, 1863. Henry (3, at two and a half years) grew up in the seven-room, white-frame house built by his father in 1861. Located at the border between Springwells and Dearborn townships in Wayne County, Michigan, the house grew with the family. An illustration (4) of the Ford farm appeared in the Historical Atlas of Wayne County, Michigan, in 1876, the same year Ford's mother died unexpectedly. To 13-year-old Henry, "the house was like a watch without a mainspring."

Three years later he left Dearborn to pursue his mechanical inclinations in Detroit. After various jobs, including nearly two years at the Detroit Dry Dock Company, he came back to the farm. He lived at the homestead (5, c.1886) until his marriage on April 11, 1888, to Clara Bryant (6 and 7, 1888). Within three years, the couple moved from Dearborn Township back to Detroit. When they returned to Dearborn in 1915, to move into their new Fair Lane estate (8), their lives and the world were much changed.

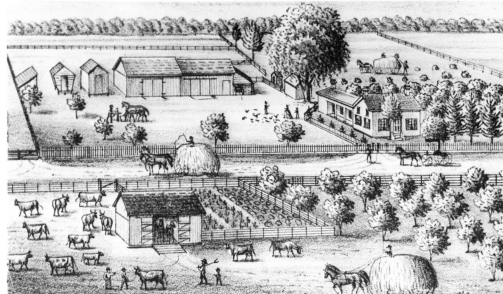

4

6   7

5

8

9

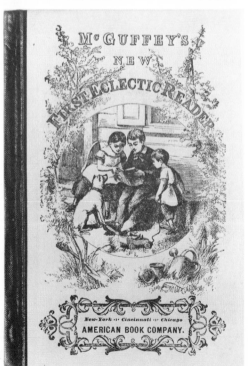

10

12

11

The Fords were living in their 12th home, located at 66 Edison Avenue in Detroit, by 1914. It was here that Clara (9, at front entrance) recalled the childhood verse, "Hear the children gaily shout / 'Half past four and school is out!'" Thinking the lines came from the first McGuffey Reader (10), Henry embarked on a search for the book that sparked his historical and collecting interests. For the rest of his life, the flame never flickered.

In a small room adjoining his Highland Park plant office, Henry Ford began to store the old treasures he had acquired. His secretary Ernest G. Liebold recalled:

> We received a great many things from people. These people would send various gifts to Mr. Ford, articles of every conceivable idea—violins, bottles with ships constructed in them and all sorts of things. They were always put into that room because Mr. Ford wanted them to be preserved.
>
> That finally became known as the "chamber of horrors," and oftentimes we wanted to clean out some of the things that were of no value or had no significance whatever, but Mr. Ford said, "Well, we're going to keep them. We're going to save them. Some day we'll put them in a museum."

Ford's pattern of saving everything had surfaced.

In 1919, 56-year-old Henry Ford's libel suit against the Chicago Tribune came to trial in Mount Clemens, Michigan. The newspapers jumped on Ford's statement that history "was bunk to me" and headlined it across the country (11, Boston Evening Transcript). The myth of Ford's disregard for history was born.

The trial proved a grueling experience for the industrialist (12). During the recesses, he found peace and relaxation in nearby farm fields (13), escaping to the soil of his past as he would so many times later in his life.

13

A Simple Beginning

Shortly after the humiliating *Chicago Tribune* trial in 1919, highway officials decided to extend Greenfield Road south through the Ford farm. However, the homestead was in the proposed road's path. The family's decision to move the house and outbuildings prompted Henry's first restoration project.

Shortly after moving the house far enough east (about 200 feet) to make way for the road, Henry asked a Ford Motor Company draftsman to design a replica of the old windmill that once stood near the barn. Ford accepted the design and found the draftsman, Edward J. Cutler, who was destined to become the architect of Ford's early American village.

After the windmill assignment, Cutler assisted with the homestead itself. Ford wanted the house restored to its condition in 1876, the year of his mother's death. The building had fallen into disrepair over the years, and most of the furnishings were hopelessly dispersed.

"When I first saw it, it was up on blocks," Cutler remembered,

> and it was just the front section, and it looked like the dickens. It was setting up about probably five feet from the ground and in a mud field. When they got it moved over and set in the place that he wanted it, why then they put a foundation under it.... The house itself, architecturally, doesn't amount to a lot. It's just a common old Michigan house; it's just as simple as could be built. But it was his home.

Ford spared nothing in furnishing the house as accurately as his memory permitted. A number of motor company employees combed the countryside, including Cutler. The latter visited almost every antique shop between Detroit and Cincinnati before he found the correct shade of worn, red carpeting for the homestead stairs. After people learned that Ford was buying antiques, his "purchasing agents" kept their identities secret.

Meanwhile, others began digging at the homestead's original site (thought to be the first archaeological dig conducted in the preservation of a historic house) to help with the research. Fred L. Black vividly recalled the experience:

> Everything they found, nails and pieces of dishes and what have you, was brought to him, and he would recognize or show them to his brothers and sisters.... In that way, he was able to find the design of dishes they had. As a result, he was able to have them reproduced.
>
> I remember one time they brought over an old pair of rusty skates. Mr. Ford recognized these skates as his own when he was a boy. I remember his great delight. I don't think he could have been given anything in the world that would have pleased him quite as much as those old, rusty skates.

The bulk of the restoration and refurnishing (much of which Ford personally participated in or directed) was completed by 1926. The restored house became a "plaything for Mr. and Mrs. Ford," according to Cutler. "They'd have parties over there, and they'd get all dressed up. The men and women were in the old costumes, and they'd dance, and they'd have their orchestra over there." Relatives and a few old friends usually constituted the guest list in those years. Roy Schumann, a motor company carpenter and woodworker, remembered Ford's hosting such an event even before finishing the house:

> In '24 or '25, he had a dance party in that barn on Halloween night. He had it decorated all up with corn stalks and everything like that, and he even put heat in the barn. We put radiators in there, and we sat out back of the barn, firing the steam engine to furnish steam for the radiators while they had the dance in the barn. I believe that was about one of the first dances that he had of the old-time square dances.

Ford also enjoyed "working" in the past. Schumann, who eventually spent most of his time at The Edison Institute, recalled: "He'd take the old equipment out and thresh. He often used to do that down at the homestead. He would invite some of the old-timers who were still around the neighborhood, and they'd watch him thresh. Mr. Ford would go over and meet them, talk with them, and different things like that."

Ford's first restoration project, ironically, would be the last building he moved to Greenfield Village.

14

The homestead looked fairly settled 200 feet east of its original site. The new Greenfield Road ran just west of the barns, which Ford dismantled (14, c.1920) and moved to their 1876 positions, relative to the house.

A 1931 post-restoration aerial view (15) makes an interesting comparison to the 1876 atlas view on page 5. By 1931, the roads were paved. Three years later, the barn across Ford Road traveled to the Chicago World's Fair (to house a soybean exhibit) and then to Greenfield Village. Cutler's windmill stood prominently in the homestead's side yard (16).

15

16

Inside (17 and 18), Ford had achieved the lived-in look he desired. Homestead dance parties inspired the guests to don old-fashioned clothes, which hung in a restored upstairs bedroom. The ladies posed for a photograph during a November 1923 function (19). Clara Ford is seated second from the left.

18

17

19

10

"My Smithsonian Institute"

In 1921, after the Ford Motor Company had transferred its tractor operations from Oakwood Boulevard to the Rouge manufacturing facility, Henry Ford moved his steadily growing hoard of antiques out of his office and into Building 13, one of the vacated assembly areas. This building stood even after a new engineering laboratory nearly encircled it in late 1924. Building 13 served as a halfway house for Ford's collection of Americana until a year or two after The Edison Institute Museum's dedication in 1929.

Harold M. Cordell, one of Ford's secretaries, assumed responsibility for handling all the incoming correspondence from people wishing to give or sell antiques to his boss. "The number of letters was *so* great," according to Cordell,

> and the fact that it was practically a one-man job made it impossible to cover the ground thoroughly. I tried my best to read all of the ... letters ... even though there were thousands of them daily. A glance would tell you what was in it or whether they were good or not. I got to be such an expert at it that I could photograph a letter with my eyes and take in the page at a glance.

During the period Building 13 served as a storehouse, there was little, if any, organized buying of antiques. Either the public sent objects, or Ford or one of his assistants picked up interesting items found while engaged in other business.

Artifacts came in all sizes. The city of Williamsburg, Virginia, for example, in 1924 offered itself to Ford for $5 million. Hoping to find someone interested in restoring dozens of historic buildings on their original site, city representative Dr. W. A. R. Goodwin commented: "For some time I've cherished the hope that Mr. Ford might be and doubtlessly would be interested in making a contribution to the United States of the old colonial capital city of Virginia." Ford, busy with his own projects, declined involvement. (The project was later backed by John D. Rockefeller, Jr.)

Cordell later estimated that in 1924 Ford was spending one or two days a week dabbling in antiques. He "dabbled" in a big way, however. Cordell remembered that:

I [never saw] him bargaining with someone on antiques. He would look at a thing and evince some interest in it, and later on, we would go around and pick it up.

There *were* times when he would go into an antique shop, and go around and point at various objects, and order them sent to Dearborn. In fact, he cleaned out two or three shops that way personally.

One might say he did quite a little buying himself when he went into an antique shop. Whatever he liked, he would say, "Pack it up and send it."

He might have realized that he was paying for the privilege of buying, himself, rather than having an anonymous agent do it. Too, a lot of times these people didn't know he was Henry Ford. It was quite amusing sometimes to see their consternation and regret when they found out who bought the goods.

Ford made decisions on what to accept or reject at Building 13 with the counsel of his personal secretary, Frank Campsall. However, no records of incoming material existed, other than correspondence between the seller or donor and one of Ford's secretaries.

The objects themselves fit every description. Threshing machines and other farm equipment arrived first, but after the homestead restoration got into full swing, furniture began to pour in as well. Guns, steam engines and cars also jammed the building. Ford described the intent of his collection: "We have no Egyptian mummies here, nor any relics of the Battle of Waterloo nor do we have any curios from Pompeii, for everything we have is strictly American."

Things "strictly American" covered a lot of ground. Workers hung large items from the rafters, stacked smaller ones on makeshift benches and racks and packed watches and clocks in bushel baskets. Relocating objects soon became a problem, as Ed Cutler learned. One day Ford asked him to find three Civil War drums stored in the building. After looking literally high and low, Cutler in desperation had a local music dealer make three such drums. After their delivery, Cutler discovered the originals hanging from the rafters.

The place Ford called "my Smithsonian Institute" and aides called "the curio shop" bustled with activity. Everything had to be in working order, so

11

those items needing repair received attention when they came in. Fred Miller, a workman later employed in The Edison Institute Museum, was rather hard on the antiques, according to Cutler.

> He was a rough son-of-a-gun, you know, to handle delicate antiques. For instance, there were pictures that came in from Wayside Inn, photographs and beautiful things, and it broke my heart to see him piling those frames up like cordwood. All that gold and stuff on them, you know. He didn't really feel the value of these things. He had been a laboring man—an awful fine fellow, though.

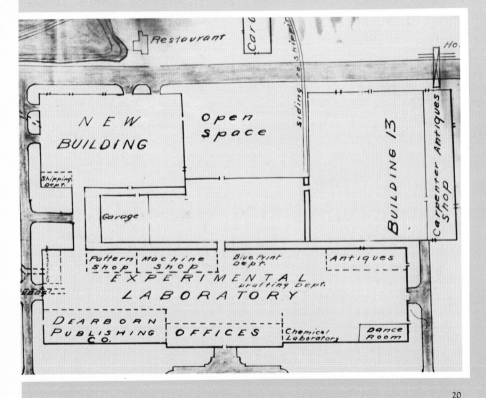

20

Cutler was given office space among the artifacts so that he could examine the pieces that came in and decide how they should look. Craftsmen on loan from Ford automotive plants then performed the actual restoration work. While valuable items usually came with authentication, most of the material did not. Sometimes the Engineering Department's library files yielded an old magazine drawing of the object, but most often "you just used a lot of horse sense" when restoring, according to Cutler. Once finished, "you would shove them over to the side," Cutler continued, and begin work on the next item. C. J. Smith restored cars in Building 13. He observed:

> All of those old cars were rebuilt better than new. We even had new tires made for them. Where they didn't have molds, they made new molds for tires, just like they used to use on them. When . . . there would be a part missing, we would make it up. But we'd make it up like it originally was. Mr. Ford showed a lot of interest in this work; he was always around.

Routinely, Ford had his men put bright, shiny new finishes on all the old furniture. Cordell (and later, noted antique furniture dealer Israel Sack, from whom Ford bought many pieces) talked him out of it, explaining that "the patina would have been spoiled, and their value reduced to nothing."
Cordell remembered that Ford

> entertained a great number of visitors here [the Engineering Laboratory], and he would always take them down to see the collection; that was part of the routine. Every time some dignitary would come in, they would walk down through there and talk over their own business at the same time. He had favorite spots and pieces all picked out, and would lead them from one to the other, and gave them a little dissertation on this one and that one, and they would go away perfectly happy. He liked the music boxes and odds and ends like the lighting fixtures.

Thomas Edison visited rather frequently. Another guest, novelist and poet Hamlin Garland, was awestruck by what he saw:

> Here, for example, stood all the successive types of reaping machines, from the hickory-fingered cradle to the latest self-binder. In another place the various types of threshing machines and horse-powers were ranged. In a third room every type of lantern, lamp, clock, gun, stove and kettle was to be seen. Every stage of American pioneer life was suggested by this exhibit. It was impossible to examine even a hundredth part of what this storehouse contained.

Soon the clutter almost overwhelmed the old building. Fortunately, a sparkling new 14-acre structure was being built a few yards away.

12

Frank Campsall

Chas Newton
1928

Henry Ford

A 1925-26 floor plan of the new Dearborn Engineering Laboratory (20) showed Building 13, the remains of the tractor plant, at the upper right with its adjoining restoration area. Henry Ford and his staff frequented the restaurant at the top of the drawing until a new dining facility was installed in the lab building. The front section of the building labeled "Antiques" is believed to have been Mrs. Ford's private exhibit area. Here she assembled items of an exceptional nature: ceramics, organs, music boxes and other varied objects. Although she seldom visited the room herself, the staff conducted tours of the area to show what could be done with the material in the larger room. In the "dance room," Ford stationed his old-time orchestra, sometimes joining the music-making. In 1925 he opened a dancing school in the room, led by dancing master Benjamin B. Lovett.

Shipments of antiques arrived almost daily at the Engineering Laboratory, some by boxcar-full, others as manageable as one in 1928 (21, left to right: Ford's secretary Frank Campsall; Charles Newton, a Ford lawyer who handled many of the village buildings business transactions; and Ford).

When Thomas Edison visited, Ford rarely missed an opportunity to show him his latest acquisitions (22, left to right: Edison's son, Charles; Ford; Edison; and Jim Bishop, Ford's collector of electrical apparatus, in 1928).

Building 13 housed an incredible variety of Americana (23).

25

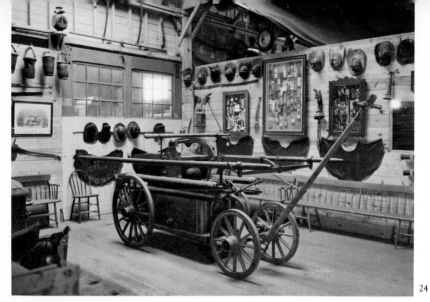

Mock-ups for village buildings underwent construction here, including, c. 1930, a carriage and wheel shop and a fire hall (24). Note the covered airplane hanging near the roof. By 1929 Ford had collected some real gems (25, a c. 1880 carved wooden cigar store Indian, "Seneca John"; 26, a c. 1760-80 Chippendale card table owned by John Hancock; 27 and 28, George Washington's camp chest and bed; 29, a c. 1810 Conestoga wagon; 30, the 1925 Fokker Tri-Motor which Admiral Richard Byrd flew over the North Pole; and 31, Henry Ford's first car, the 1896 Quadricycle).

24

30

27

29

31

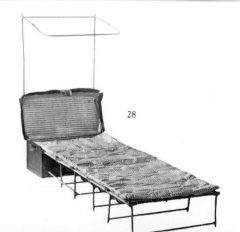

28

26

Further Tales of the Wayside Inn

In 1923, Henry Ford purchased the Wayside Inn, its outbuildings and 90 acres of surrounding land for $65,000. To insure the character of its environment, Ford bought an additional 2,500 acres and began to put together a restored village of farms and schools to enhance the inn. He even spent $330,000 to move the Boston Post Road and its growing traffic problems away from the inn. While his activity in the project waned in 1926-27 when he began to build Greenfield Village, Ford and his friends still periodically visited the restored inn whose doors had opened to the public. In the tradition of the inn's early days, Ford paid for the room and board of traveling clergymen.

Ford responded to people's questions (especially in Massachusetts) about his intentions with an article in the July 1926 issue of *Garden & Home Builder* magazine, entitled "Why I Bought the Wayside Inn and What I am Doing With It." He explained:

> The Wayside Inn, at South Sudbury, Massachusetts, is one of the oldest in the country — we are a new country and nothing is very old, but the Wayside Inn has housed George Washington and the Marquis de Lafayette and, through Longfellow's "Tales of a Wayside Inn," has become a part of the nation. It is something that ought to be preserved for all the time for the public, and when it came up for sale we bought it, not at all as a personal matter, but to preserve for the public. The Inn expressed the pioneer spirit — and the pioneer spirit is what America has, over and above any other country. If ever we lose that spirit, if ever we get to the point where a majority of the people are afraid to do things because no one before them has done them or because they are hard to do, then we shall stop going forward and start to go back.

> I deeply admire the men who founded this country, and I think we ought to know more about them and how they lived and the force and courage they had. Of course, we can read about them, but even if the account we are reading happens to be true, and often it is not, it cannot call up the full picture.

> At first we had no intention of doing more than buying the inn and restoring it. But, since it is on a public road, there was nothing at all to prevent it from being exploited and the roads lined for half a mile around with peanut and hot-dog stands, and side shows, and all sorts of catch-penny places. We had to preserve the setting, and so we bought enough additional land for that. Now we are moving the road because the jarring threatens the Inn's foundations.

> There was a good deal to be done. The Inn had been considerably modernized. We tore out the brick work which had closed up many of the old fireplaces, and now we have sixteen big fireplaces — some of them big enough to hold logs that take three men to lift. We have restored the floors.

> The lighting gave us a good deal of trouble. The old inn was lighted by candles in wall sconces and in candlesticks. These had been replaced by ordinary electric-light fixtures. We could not, as a practical matter, go back to candlelight, for the fire risk would have been too great. We finally managed to get sconces such as must have been used in the inn, and to get candle-shaped electric lights which very well imitate the old candles.

> Then we went out to find some of the relics of the inn which had disappeared. Most of them we have found. One trunk, for instance, we located and brought back from Kansas. The old Bible we managed to repair, and we put it in a case so that it will last for ever. The old clock had not been running for many years. It was made in England in 1710, and many of the parts were badly worn, although other parts, in spite of all the years of service, were as good as new. We made new parts to replace the worn ones, but we saved all of the old parts and have them in a case fastened inside the clock.

> Thus, bit by bit, we have the Inn about as it was when Washington first stayed there during the Revolution. The furniture did not give us much trouble. We had rather a large collection of New England furniture of the period, and the inn itself had a great many fine pieces which only needed expert repairing.

> Furnishing the Wayside Inn started us on the way to collecting old furniture and carts and every object used in this country during and since Colonial times. That collection has grown until now it covers several acres in one of our buildings at Dearborn. It is not as yet an ordered collection. One of these days the collection will be put into a museum.

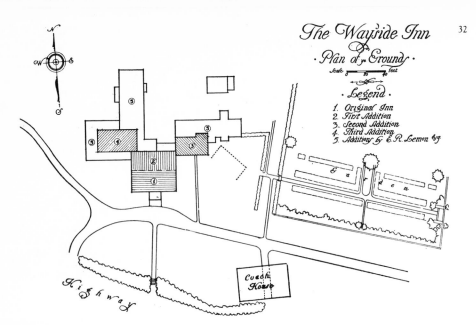

The Wayside Inn
· Plan of Ground ·
Scale

· Legend ·
1. Original Inn
2. First Addition
3. Second Addition
4. Third Addition
5. Addition by E.R. Lemon Esq

The Wayside Inn had quite a history, even after Henry Wadsworth Longfellow immortalized it in 1863. First known as the Red Horse Tavern, the inn outlasted the large oak tree bearing its signboard, thanks in great measure to Edward R. Lemon, who bought it in 1897. Lemon not only restored the deteriorating exterior and interior and opened it up once again to the public, but added other structures at the rear, a front and side porch and dormers (32 and 33).

After Lemon's death in 1919, his widow could not handle the inn alone. The new owner, Henry Ford, retained Lemon's additions and engaged Israel Sack, a prominent eastern antiques dealer, to furnish the interior. Within two weeks, Sack had the basic pieces installed. He sent Ford a bill and was promptly paid for his services, although the automaker did not view the job until a year later.

By 1926, much of the inn's restoration was complete (34, an upstairs bedroom). Ford and his friends danced to old-fashioned music in the ballroom, one of the inn's later additions. One such dance in 1926 honored Alice Longfellow, the poet's daughter (35, Longfellow in front center, with cane; at far left, Benjamin Lovett).

Clara almost invariably accompanied Henry on trips to the Wayside Inn. Family and friends were always welcome (36, Ford, Harvey Firestone and Thomas Edison).

Closer to Home

Henry Ford's purchase and restoration of the 1836 Botsford Inn, 16 miles northwest of Detroit, in 1924, provided the final stepping stone to Greenfield Village and The Edison Institute Museum. The Ford Homestead got him started, the Wayside Inn served as practice for his historic village idea and the Botsford Inn restoration, at which he planned to enshrine American pioneer life, brought his efforts once again close to home. Managing such projects from a distance was proving to be an awkward and costly venture, even for Ford.

Despite the surplus colonial furnishings accumulated for the Wayside Inn project, Ford "was not misled into thinking that what is delightfully suitable in one place will surely prove equally satisfying in another," a December 1926 article in The Magazine *Antiques* pointed out.

Michigan and New England are different places, each possessing its own peculiar traditions, each harboring its own latent historical consciousness responsive to an appropriate appeal. To have translated the Botsford

Tavern into the New England vernacular would have been like substituting a model of Noah's Ark for that of the Mayflower in a Plymouth Rock pageant. Mr. Ford did not commit the error.

The restoration itself did not proceed without incident. Ed Cutler, by 1924 Ford's right-hand man on such projects, almost lost his job over the Botsford Tavern venture. Cutler related: "The stairway is and was then a very bad feature in the building. The thing that was worst about it was that every time you would go up the stairs you'd strike your head on the ceiling in the well hole." Cutler proceeded to cut the ceiling back accordingly, but "when Mr. Ford came, he didn't like that at all. He was mad, and he told me to take my tools and go on back to Dearborn. So I went back to Dearborn and I thought my time had come." Fortunately for Cutler, and for Greenfield Village, Ford cooled off and accepted a compromise on the stairway ceiling.

Harold Cordell, Ford's antiques secretary, remembered a slightly more humorous story:

When they tore down the walls to fix up one of the rooms, they found the mummy of a dead cat which had fallen behind the partition and evidently had suffocated or died of hunger. Henry had the old cat placed in a small case with a glass top and brought up to the museum, and that was one of our exhibits for a while.

Though Ford spent a lot of time on site during the restoration, according to Cutler, he soon lost interest in the Botsford Inn, except for occasional dance parties there. Ford had danced at the inn as a youth and his love of old-fashioned dancing lured him back to the tavern with his wife and friends. A maple floor was added to the ballroom and the architect felt "it was a beautiful floor and a lovely floor to dance on .... At the last dance they had, the water supply gave out," Cutler remembered. "City water wasn't out as far as Grand River Avenue at that time. As a result, all the sanitary conveniences were stopped up, and they closed Botsford Tavern."

The tavern occasionally was rented out for parties until 1934, when it once again served the public.

38

The Botsford Inn once served 19th-century travelers journeying from Detroit to Lansing. By June of 1924, when Henry Ford bought it, the entire building had dilapidated, including the front portion facing Grand River Avenue (37). In October the structure was moved 300 feet back from the highway for vibration protection and aesthetics (38). By November, Ford's reconstruction crew, led by Ed Cutler, had attached much of the siding and installed the rough outlines of the original two-story porch. One year after Ford purchased the property for $100,000 and spent an additional $336,000 on restoration, the inn presented an attractive example of 19th-century highway hospitality (39 and 40).

40

39

1927-1929

We ought to know more about the families who founded this nation, and how they lived . . . . One way to do this is to reconstruct as nearly as possible the conditions under which they lived . . . .

— HENRY FORD

Chapter Two

Construction Begins

Question: But just out of the clear sky one day, he [Ford] asked you to draw a village?
Answer: Yes.

Edward J. Cutler, "Reminiscences"

Exactly when The Edison Institute became a concrete idea in Henry Ford's mind remains hazy, but specific references appear in letters as early as 1925. *The Ladies Home Journal* made the first public mention of the complex's establishment in its September 1928 issue. Between those two dates, a flurry of activity emanated from Dearborn.

From the beginning Ford intended to have two separate facilities linked by his theories of education. A museum would tell the story of man's technological and cultural progress through comprehensive displays of inventions and artifacts. A village of early American life would show how similar objects were made and used. Ford would also preserve vanishing residential, commercial and industrial architectural forms there. In his planned school system, students would learn not only from books, but also from three-dimensional objects reflecting the American past.

The actual plans for the village began in the manner architect Edward J. Cutler cited in the oral reminiscence passage quoted above. Although Ford considered several sites, he evidently decided on the present location because of its proximity to the Engineering Laboratory and his Dearborn estate, Fair Lane. Cutler generally based his early sketches (Ford's staff artist, Irving Bacon, drew others) on New England villages, with public buildings centered around a common green.

Although Ford liked the initial plan, he changed it countless times, even after buildings were in place! Some buildings were left on blocks to make the periodic shifting easier. Architect Cutler felt Ford's March 1928 decision to

21

include a restoration of Thomas Edison's Menlo Park (New Jersey) Compound cemented the village layout. The two focal points became the village green and the Menlo Park complex. Everything else seemed to fall into place around them.

Several buildings had already arrived in the village by March of 1928. The pace of reconstruction increased considerably, however, when Ford announced that the institute's dedication would coincide with the 50th anniversary tribute to Edison's invention of the incandescent lamp. Celebration of Light's Golden Jubilee, on October 21, 1929, would center on the Menlo Park Compound in Greenfield Village. From then on, Cutler and his crews, helped by other Ford agents, constantly examined, sketched and photographed possible buildings for "the boss" to include in his village. Those chosen were measured, dismantled carefully but quickly (often with manpower supplied by local Ford dealers) and shipped to Dearborn. Working from measured drawings and, usually, labeled parts, Cutler supervised reconstruction in the village.

Building materials were painstakingly copied when originals were missing or in poor condition. Ford went to extreme lengths to insure accuracy, although at times alterations were made for specific purposes. Modern sanitary facilities, for example, became fixtures in most dwellings as Ford originally planned for 300 people to live and work in a fully operational village.

While Cutler oversaw the work, it was clearly Ford's show. He made all the decisions on what to put where. He frequently showed up on the site — almost daily at times. Cutler remembered:

> He spent so much time around the village. Several times he would make a crack, "Well, I guess I'll have to leave you now, and go and make some more money for us to spend down here."
>
> It was a relief for him to get down there. For years he wouldn't let me have a telephone. When I would ask him about it, and I had a lot of running around to do, he would say, "Oh forget that stuff. I came down here to get away from that gang." He didn't want any way for them to get a hold of him. I eventually got a telephone, but I had to ask for it a good many times . . . . On his daily routine, he always made the advances unless I'd ask him to see a certain job or thing we were doing in the village. It was entirely up to his discretion. You never knew when he was coming back. He would always leave with, "I'll see you later." It might be two days or it might be ten minutes. If he was very much interested in something I was doing, he was in there three or four times a day. His favorite area in the village was the one in hand.

Meanwhile, plans for the other elements — the museum and school system — progressed as well. On a cruise to Europe in 1928, Henry met one of son Edsel's friends, architect Robert O. Derrick. Ford asked Derrick if he had any design ideas for his proposed museum building in Dearborn. Thinking quickly, Derrick suggested reproducing Philadelphia's Independence Hall. Ford like the proposal and the museum project moved forward. Early in 1929, Ford announced a $5 million gift to build the museum. (He had already spent more than $2 million on antiques and village restorations.)

Thomas Edison signed the concrete cornerstone (while it was still wet) on September 27, 1928, shortly after Derrick had fixed the location of the proposed building. Edison also dedicated his old Fort Myers, Florida,

Laboratory that day by starting the steam engine. The lab was the first completely restored building in the village.

Actual construction on the museum began in April 1929 and the entire front section, with a replica of Independence Hall in the center and portions representing Congress Hall and Old City Hall on the ends, was finished by the October 21 dedication and celebration of Light's Golden Jublilee. The eight-acre mechanical arts hall at the back of the museum took a few more years to complete. Work on the 350,000 square feet of teakwood flooring continued as late as 1938.

About a month before the dedication ceremonies, the village school program began. Thirty-two children in grades four through seven attended their first day of class on September 16, 1929, in the old Scotch Settlement School Henry Ford had attended. At its peak, the village system would include nine school buildings, housing kindergarten through post-high school technical levels. The schools, like the village and museum themselves, offered participants a truly unique experience. And the fun was only beginning!

2

1

3

Courtesy Burton Historical Collection

4

5

Although Henry Ford (1) was the prime mover behind the creation and building of The Edison Institute, he did enjoy the help of two co-founders: his wife, Clara, and his son, Edsel (2). Ford knew what he wanted to achieve in the complex and, for the most part, did not consult professional advisors. Two architects proved notable exceptions: Edward J. Cutler (3), who built much of the village, and Robert O. Derrick (4), who designed the museum structure. Cutler came from the Ford Motor Company's ranks, as did most of the others who worked on the institute project. Derrick had his own architectural firm.

During the building and early development of the village and museum, key men either continued on the company payroll or became attached to Ford's personal staff. Harold M. Cordell (not pictured), assistant secretary to Ford from 1921 to 1929, handled antiques correspondence and helped with early assemblage of artifacts in Building 13.

James Humberstone (5), schoolboy editor of the Henry Ford Trade School student newspaper, The Artisan, became associated with Ford News and was appointed one of the first "curators" of artifacts in Building 13, even though, "I couldn't even spell the word" antiques. He continued as an aide to Ford after the museum dedication, living in the village's Sarah Jordan Boarding House with his wife while in charge of museum artifacts and exhibits.

Fred L. Black (6), staff member of the Dearborn Independent, editor of Ford News and Ford Motor Company advertising manager, acted as a general aide and liaison with the architect during museum construction. Eventually he became nominal director of the museum and a member of the institute board of trustees.

Ernest G. Liebold (7), Ford's general secretary, who exercised considerable power in the early development of the institute, oversaw the 1929 dedication ceremonies.

Frank Campsall (8), personal secretary to Ford, began as an assistant secretary under Liebold and gradually grew more influential during the 1930s. Campsall, who acted as Ford's right hand on decisions regarding village and museum purchases, also gained a place on the institute board of trustees.

William J. Cameron (9), originally a staff member of the Dearborn Independent, became the personal public relations spokesman for Henry Ford around 1921. He wrote for and about Ford and spoke at numerous village functions, chapel services and dedications.

24

6

7

9

8

11

12

10

Francis Jehl (10), former laboratory assistant to Thomas Edison, came to Dearborn to help with the restoration of the Menlo Park complex and stayed on until his death in 1941, writing memoirs and interpreting the Edison buildings for guests and visitors.

Both Herbert F. Morton (11) and James W. Bishop (12) collected heavily for Ford. Morton, an Englishman, acquired an extensive array of early steam engines and various other artifacts, including the Cotswold buildings. When Ford first asked Morton in 1928 if it would be possible to put together a complete collection of steam power apparatus from the earliest days, Morton replied that yes, enough examples still existed, but "the cost . . . would be enormous." Ford answered: "Well, I'll tell you—I'll spend $10 million." Bishop, superintendent of substations for the Detroit Edison Company, gathered items associated with generating, conducting, controlling and using electricity. Ford wanted at least one of every such device ever made.

25

From Field to Village

While Ford's agents busily collected artifacts for the future museum, Ford and Ed Cutler (*13, at the village in 1929*) planned the village layout. An aerial view (*14*) taken in October 1927 shows that the institute's future site — between the large building in the left foreground and the river in the left background — was basically open land. The building in the foreground is the Ford Engineering Laboratory. Building 13, the square ribbed-roof portion, visible at the right, was then full of antiques of every description. Toward the center of the picture sat the recently completed Ford Airport and at top center, a dirigible mooring mast. The museum building would rise in the triangle of open land directly to the right of the rectangular torn-up area behind Building 13.

Ford and Cutler decided on this site in late 1926. Cutler later said,

I remember walking over that property where the village is at the present time. It was just a field. Then there was an old road that went through there with some old trees and a couple of houses on it, one on top of the old knoll there, where Jimmy Humberstone lived. We walked up the old road.

Then he took me over to Cherry Hill, on the end of the Cherry Hill Road there where the golf links are now, and we walked all over that property, considered it as a village project. There wasn't the chance for

development over there, and it was separate from all the activities of the company. This present location was much more favorable. I know he liked that better.

That "old road" was Duffield Road (*15*), now called South Dearborn Road in Greenfield Village. Within three years of Cutler's and Ford's initial visit, it would begin to earn its nickname, "America's residential row," with the installation of its first historic house.

By early 1927, when Cutler started drawing sketches of proposed villages, Ford owned four historic buildings that could be included in the plan: Thomas Edison's Fort Myers (Florida) Laboratory, the Clinton (Michigan) Inn, the Waterford (Michigan) Country Store and the Scotch Settlement (Dearborn Township, Michigan) School.

None of these buildings (all waiting on their original sites), however, was the deciding factor in the placement of the central village green. Rather, the position of the church (which Cutler would design) determined the location of the green. In traditional American town plans, the church stood on the highest ground. In the village this meant the knoll above the old Rouge River bed. The green would extend from the church, with the other public buildings grouped around the common ground in the manner of a typical New England town. No one town was copied. "It was your impression," Cutler said, "it was purely imaginative."

On the fringes of the green and its planned church, town hall, school, inn and general store, would sit other functioning buildings necessary to a village's existence: homes, shops, post office, fire station, doctor's office, factories and so on.

Although Cutler recommended, clearly Ford made all the decisions. "That commons was a very valuable piece of ground," Cutler remembered.

We always had something better to put around it. It was taken up that way. That ground that is around the commons, I planned dozens of things to go into various open spots around there. We always held that that was the best spot. We always wanted the best buildings there. We wanted to be careful what we put there.

In October of 1927, Henry Ford's vision and planning for a collective setting in which to interpret America's vibrant past became a reality. Construction commenced.

13

15

14

The first building to arrive at the village site was the 1854 *Waterford Country Store* from the small town of that name, located 30 miles northwest of Detroit. Purchased in August 1927 with the proviso that Ford would build a new brick structure for the owner, the store was raised off its foundation, ready for dismantling, that same month (16). The planned village subsequently received its first raw materials in October. Cutler's men re-erected the store during the winter, but did not put it on its foundation facing the village green until the spring of 1929 as Ford often moved the early buildings until he was satisfied with their placement.

Before he acquired the country store, Ford had purchased the *Clinton Inn* from Ella Smith, who still lived in the badly deteriorated structure. "There was only one man in 4,000 that would consider it anything but a pile of junk," Cutler said, and the only way "to explain what it looked like . . . is to look at the pictures" (17, c. 1925).

Interior conditions were worse (18). The original barroom provided the only livable space. Cutler expressed amazement at the mess. "She had it filled with newspapers and magazines in that room . . . . I found magazines there older than I was, just

16

17

piled up in piles! There were bottles of milk there—I'll bet you they were ten years old—that had never been opened, and eggs and stuff around." Cutler incurred Smith's wrath by kicking over two buckets of water on the porch—water she washed her hair in. Harold Cordell tackled the job of moving Smith out and Cutler attended to moving the building to Greenfield Village.

"When we brought it in, the village plan hadn't been completed," Cutler related.

> The first thing was to get the building together again, the main section. There was no attempt to put it on a foundation in the first spot. It was just put on skids because they weren't satisfied with the location. Then after Mr. Ford made up his mind as to the permanent location, we got it on the spot, the foundation in under it, and really went after it to finish it up. Mr. Ford showed a lot of interest in this particular building.

Cutler's crew finished the restoration in the spring of 1929 (19), almost a year and a half after the dismantling. Where possible, original materials were reused, such as the hand-hewn floor beams. By the end of August, the building, lacking only shutters and landscaping, appeared ready to receive dedication dignitaries (20, next to Waterford Store).

The original rustic elegance returned to the barroom, including an array of spirit bottles lining the wall shelves (21). The permanence of the bottles, however, was not a sure thing, as Ford biographer and village public relations man William A. Simonds remembered:

> A very interesting thing happened about that inn at the time that the village opened. . . . There were shelves along the wall behind the bar and Fred Smith and some of the others from the museum brought down bottles and put them along the shelves, to make it look like a bar. Mr. Ford came in and I was with him at the time. He was making an inspection and he said, "Where did those bottles come from?" I said, "They're from the museum." He said, "Well, what are they doing up here?" I said, "Well, they're to make the barroom look more realistic." "Well," he said, "I want them taken out of here, removed out. I don't want any whiskey bottles in here." So I had to get Fred to come up and get the bottles out.
>   Well, then Mrs. Ford and Mrs. Edison came along. She was very proud of Clinton Inn and she was showing Mrs. Edison and she looked in the barroom and there were no bottles. So she sent word down to the museum to get the bottles up there before the big day. So back came the bottles. Then Mr. Ford came in again. He saw them there, and he said, "I thought I said to have those bottles removed." I said, "Well, they were removed." He said, "Who said to put them back?" And I said, "Mrs. Ford." He said, "Okay," and that's all there was to it. So they've been there ever since.

18   19

20

21

29

As early as 1925 Ford arranged to ship Thomas Edison's Fort Myers, Florida, laboratory/workshop to Dearborn. Since the Fords and Edisons had winter cottages in Fort Myers, often vacationing together after 1914 (22, c. 1925), Henry knew the structure well. Edison used the laboratory, built in 1884-85, for more than 40 winters, beginning with his honeymoon trip in 1886.

When Ford first asked about acquiring the building in May 1925, Edison's assistant, William H. Meadowcroft, replied:

> Mr. Edison's attention has just been called to this letter and he wishes me to say to you that Mr. Ford can have the old laboratory building at any time, as Mr. Edison can put up a smaller building for a motor generator for charging his batteries and also to serve as a garage for his automobile.

The Edisons' decision to take a vacation and Ford's failure to complete a replacement building delayed plans to move it during the winter of 1925-26. Edison then became involved with rubber experiments and needed the lab. Finally, by early summer 1928, with necessary equipment moved to the new building, dismantling of the original began (23).

Ford asked Roy Schumann to "have some of the men cut the grass and clean it up because he was going to put up Edison's Fort Myers Laboratory" on a spot he had chosen in the village. "We cleared a space about 150 feet wide and about 100 feet long," Schumann said. "Some days later a car came in with the material, and we unloaded it and put it down there. That was all shipped in by railroad. Everything was identified, and we piled it so we could reach certain parts first, and then construction was started later."

Henry Ford took considerable interest in this project, checking in frequently during construction (24, at right, on September 14, one week before the building's completion). Several motives probably prompted Ford's attention: it was the first building finished; it was associated with his friend and hero, Edison; and it would be the site, on September 27, 1928, of the village's first dedication ceremony.

30

22

23

25

24

Edison came to the village on that blustery, cold September day to start up the lab's engine (25), a symbolic beginning to Ford's dream. Later in the day, Edison dedicated the cornerstone of the museum.

Once officially acknowledged by Edison's act, the village building program seemed to jump into full gear. A number of structures arrived on the site in 1928, and were worked on into the next year.

The 1885 Addison Ford Barn (26, on its original site and 27, in the village), located on the property of Ford's second cousin near the Ford homestead, served as the Clinton Inn's livery and stabled horses ridden by village schoolchildren.

The 1906 Luther Burbank Office, originally positioned in one corner of Burbank's 40-acre experimental gardens in Santa Rosa, California (28), would occupy several spots in Greenfield Village. Just prior to the 1929 dedication, it could be seen behind the trees on old Duffield Road (29, at right), the road Henry Ford renamed South Dearborn. By 1935, the structure stood across the road, above the banks of the Rouge River.

26

27

28

29

Deluge Fire House, erected mid-19th-century, arrived from Newton, New Hampshire, in 1928. The building, like the Burbank Office and a number of other structures, remained on skids for several years to facilitate its moving (30).

Built in 1828, the Whittier Tollhouse/Shoeshop moved from the banks of the Merrimack River in East Haverhill, Massachusetts, to a former bridge tender's backyard when the bridge it served was torn down in 1911. Ford had the 10-foot-by-12-foot building shipped to Greenfield Village in 1928, and it, too, changed locations. To pass idle time, many toll collectors became shoemakers. This dual function continued in the village as Henry Ford had a craftsman in the shop make his shoes for a number of years. Today, it once more stands mute guard to a water crossing, the village's Ackley Covered Bridge (31).

30

31

America's Greatest Preservation

In March 1928, Henry Ford decided to restore Thomas Edison's entire Menlo Park, New Jersey, "invention factory" in Greenfield Village. That decision not only foretold a tremendous undertaking in itself, but also offered an anchor for the numerous buildings already floating on the site. The village green and the Menlo Park complex became the central points around which the other buildings revolved. Ford wanted to reconstruct Menlo Park in every detail, including directional orientation. Once the buildings shared the same alignment with the compass that they had in New Jersey, their location in the village became set. Ford now embarked on what would be called the greatest and most significant single preservation effort in America, possibly even the world.

Contemporary observer and Ford aide William Simonds described the story of that preservation in his 1938 publication, *Henry Ford and Greenfield Village:*

> By then the two friends had discussed Mr. Ford's plans and Edison was familiar with what was in the other's mind. Together they visited the deserted site of Menlo Park in New Jersey, where for nearly ten years after 1876 the inventor had toiled, giving to the world the telephone transmitter, phonograph, incandescent lamp, and all the foundations of electric current distribution.
>
> They found the large frame laboratory had been dismantled by neighboring farmers for the lumber salvage it contained. A few brick foundations marked the spot where the machine-shop had stood. Working from these first clues and with Edison's ready assistance, Mr. Ford directed the reclaiming and regathering of materials for the restoration of the Menlo Park buildings.
>
> Some of the original boards were found stored by a farmer. Others were regained through purchase of sheds and other farm buildings. Excavating on the grounds (which Mr. Ford had acquired), diggers brought to light a vast array of relics from Edison's day, ranging from underground wiring for the first electric railroad built there by him in 1880 to the old dump pile where the former workmen had thrown broken and discarded objects. Here was a treasure find such as would have gladdened the heart of an archaeologist. All was carefully gathered together and shipped to Dearborn, even the broken bottles and shards.
>
> Carloads of red New Jersey clay from the old grounds, together with rocks for foundations, were shipped. Nothing was overlooked, not even the stump of the old hickory tree that once grew near the laboratory.
>
> Mr. Ford sought Edison's advice as to the best source to whom he could go for accurate information concerning the layout of the buildings and furnishings. Edison suggested Mr. Francis Jehl, a former assistant who had worked in the laboratory in 1878-9 and for a time in the early 80s, until he was sent abroad by the inventor to assist in introducing the Edison system in Europe. Mr. Jehl was asked to come to Dearborn and oversee the restoration, and agreed.
>
> The boarding-house near the laboratory where Mr. Jehl and other workmen lived was found intact at Menlo Park, purchased, and dismantled for restoration in a corresponding location in the Village.
>
> Of the two-story brick building that served as office building and library, only one shutter could be found. Mr. Ford arranged to have bricks supplied by the firm furnishing the original ones, and after the structure had been built, placed a single slat from the original shutter in each of those shading the windows of the new office-library.
>
> One building complete in its original features was recovered. It was the little photographic studio in which bulbs for the first successful lamps were blown, and later became known as the "little glass house." It had been located some years previously by the General Electric Company and placed as a shrine in one of the employees' parks. At a ceremony attended by Mr. Edison, the company presented the house to Mr. Ford.
>
> Remnants of the original electric locomotive built by Edison in Menlo Park in 1880 were given by the company, and Mr. Ford set men at work restoring it, as well as duplicating the two small cars it had hauled.

The six buildings forming the Menlo Park Compound —
laboratory, glass house, carbon shed, carpenter shop,
library / office and machine shop — have led varied existences.
During Edison's tenure, 1876-85, the 1¼-acre complex
hummed with activity (32, the machine shop, c. 1880).
Edison obtained patents for more than 420 inventions during
this period, including the phonograph and the incandescent
lamp and lighting system. Many believe his establishment of the
world's first industrial research facility at Menlo Park carries
the greatest significance of all his creative efforts.

After Edison and his operation left, the buildings suffered
various fates (33, library / office). By the time Ford decided to
move what remained, some had been adapted for other uses.
Materials stripped from some of the buildings appeared in other
structures nearby.

An associated building, the c. 1870 Sarah Jordan Boarding
House, remained nearly intact as did the small structure in
which glass bulbs were blown. The General Electric Company
had preserved the latter building in an employees' park at
Parsippany, New Jersey.

32

33

34

Little remained of the other structures as Ford, Edison and the latter's son Charles discovered (34, c. 1928). What did remain was further dismantled for transfer.

Reconstruction depended upon original drawings, original photographs (from which bricks, for instance, could be counted) and the memories of some of the "old-timers." By December 1928, the boarding house approached its final form next to the Fort Myers Laboratory (35). Foundations for the other buildings stood in various stages of construction. By the end of January 1929, the basic frames of the main lab and machine shop were finished, but the office/library was still barely above ground level (36).

35

36

37

38

40

36

39

41

42

Seven boxcar-loads of New Jersey clay were spread over the compound in the early spring (37).

From Ford Airport, the Menlo Park panorama presented an impressive sight on April 26 (38). Reproductions of lab chairs were some of the first furnishings (39, original chair at left).

The complex neared completion when a crew paved the road adjacent to the village during the late summer or early fall of 1929 (40). Inside the lab (41) all was set for the re-creation of Edison's incandescent lamp experiment during Light's Golden Jubilee on October 21. By Christmas, covered with newly fallen snow, the compound bore the settled look of a long-time Michigan resident (42, December 20, 1929).

43

44

45

38

While Menlo Park rose out of the fields along the new Village Road, a number of other historic structures claimed their places in the layout.

Henry Ford purchased the 1832 Loranger Grist Mill, located on Stony Creek near Monroe, Michigan (43), in January 1928. It was one of the few structures moved to the village without prior disassembly. Ford added a wing during its reconstruction in the village to house the new power source: a steam engine and boiler.

Operated in Phoenixville, Connecticut, as both an apothecary shop and post office, the c. 1830 Phoenixville Post Office caught the eye of Ford agent William Taylor, and dismantling began in September 1928 (44). The hand-split laths that held the plaster in place were clearly visible. By the time of the October 21 dedication, the completed post office (45) carried official registry and its own postmark. The first mail to come through was a special delivery letter for President Herbert Hoover. More than 600 letters for Thomas Edison also arrived that day.

Ford's admiration of Edison, his childhood hero, sparked his acquisition of the 1858 Smiths Creek Station. During Ford's winter 1928-29 Florida visit, Edison related that as a boy he had been thrown off a Grand Trunk Western train at the Smiths Creek (Michigan) Depot for accidentally setting fire to the baggage compartment. Ford decided to see if the station still existed. He found it in decent shape (46, Ford's grandchildren, Benson, left, and Henry II, standing outside the station in March 1929) and negotiated with the town and Grand Trunk for its removal to the village (47), agreeing to build a replacement (48). The original building was then positioned on a spur near the Michigan Central tracks that ran along the north edge of the village. The completed structure played a featured role in the dedication when it received the honored guests traveling by special train from the Rouge plant station.

46

47

48

49

Henry Ford and his father used to bring raw wool to the c. 1850 Plymouth Carding Mill for processing into rovings, which were then taken home for spinning into thread or yarn. Still on its original site west of Dearborn on the Middle Rouge River in May 1929 (49), the building received Ed Cutler's usual supervision during its removal and reconstruction in Greenfield Village. Initial work revealed what Cutler termed "barn-frame" construction (50). The job was completed by early September.

Cutler inspected and sketched the 1845 Plymouth House, a simplified Greek Revival building with return cornices (Ford's favorite style of architecture), in early June 1929. Removal proved swift (51) and workmen were painting the house on its new village site near the Clinton Inn by August 22 (52).

Dismantling of the 1832 Gardner House, located in the Scotch Settlement area of Dearborn Township, commenced in April 1929. In one of the rare instances in which a camera recorded Henry Ford on a project site, he watched (53, on the ground at left, in topcoat and hat) as a subsequent addition's chimney was toppled. Later, he climbed to the roof for a better view. Before work had begun, Ford visited the site

40

51

and recounted the experience to aide Jimmy Humberstone:

> This morning I was by a home called the Gardner
> House, where as a boy I used to frequently stop when I
> was coming back from Detroit at a late hour. Rather
> than go on to the house and disturb my father, I would
> sleep with the Gardner boys. This morning I was by
> that house because we plan on moving it to the historic
> village we are about to build. I found some marbles, put
> a few in the palm of my hand, and as I applied pressure,
> they disintegrated. Life, change, had gone on.

The dwelling was at the village and roughed in by early June
next to a building about ten years older, but similar in basic
design, the Pioneer Log Cabin (**54,** Gardner House at right).
The cabin, originally located about a quarter of a mile from the
Ford homestead, had been occupied by an old acquaintance of
Ford. Cutler recalled the move to the village: "I can't
remember clearly, but it seems to me that thing was carted over
here. They probably opened the roof up and flopped it down,
and carted the whole works over here on a big truck, without
tearing it apart. . . . I cannot remember that thing being torn to
pieces." Both structures were in place for the dedication
ceremonies.

52

54

55   56

57

Although the Scotch Settlement School in Dearborn was one of Ford's first purchases (1923), it did not arrive in the village until the summer of 1929. Ford had attended the school himself and revisited it occasionally in intervening years (55, seated at right, c. 1906). He operated experimental pre-school classes in the red brick building after restoration on its original site, which began in 1923. During that job, the crew rebuilt the back wall about an inch and a half out of line. Cutler instructed the plasterer to apply more plaster to make it look straight. Typically, Henry Ford happened along and noticed something wrong. Cutler told him what he planned to do and Ford replied, "To hell with that! Tear the damn thing down." The entire wall was rebuilt and Cutler admitted, "That's one time I made a poor judgment." As the two worked together more and more on dozens of buildings, Cutler came to appreciate Ford's desire for accuracy.

Scarcely a month before the building itself was moved to the village in June 1929, a tree preceded it (56). Reconstruction began immediately and workmen were putting on the roof, minus cupola, by the first week in July. On September 16, 1929, about a month before the formal dedication of the entire Edison Institute, 32 students in the first through fourth grades began full-time classes at the Scotch Settlement School with a greeting from Henry Ford (57). This event launched a fascinating combination of progressive, one-room school education and "learning-by-doing."

58

59

60

61

Ford wanted a building with a Lincoln connection, but they were hard to come by in 1929. Abraham Lincoln practiced law in Postville, Illinois' 1840 Logan County Courthouse .early in his career. By 1848, the county seat had moved to a different town, and the courthouse served various ensuing roles: post office, general store, school, jail and, finally, when Henry Ford's agents discovered it in 1929, a private home (58). The forgotten and dilapidated building (59, indications of original chimney on right wall) caused a furor, however, when townspeople heard Ford had purchased it for removal to his village. They suddenly became interested and tried, through the courts, to keep the structure in Postville. Ford, however, owned the building. He sent Cutler and crew to Illinois and, as Cutler recalled,

> That job was one of those hurry up things, and we took a bunch of men down there. We followed my measurements through as quickly as possible but had the men building a fence around the thing. The first day we had the fence around the thing and the roof off. I got wind of some gang of people getting an injunction against us to stop it because they realized that we were going to cart that thing away to Greenfield Village. By the time they had their legal end of it taken care of, we had the walls and whole thing flattened to the ground and were carting it off. We beat them to it. The injunction was the main reason for the hurry up deal.

A number of years later, the state of Illinois built a replica of the building on the original site.

Once in the village, the newly named Lincoln Courthouse went up almost as fast as it had come down. Ford wanted it completed for the October 21 dedication. Dismantling had started in Illinois on September 8. By September 26, workers were building a foundation in the village, facing the green next to the Scotch Settlement School (60). Less than a month later, the building was ready to receive Ford's 400 guests (61).

43

62

64

63

Although a few other structures lay in pieces somewhere on the property by the dedication day (notably the 1750 Secretary Pearson House from Exeter, New Hampshire, and the 1860 Chapman House from Dearborn Township), no other historic buildings from original locations were added to the village scene until after the ceremonies.

Early in 1929, "architect" Ford either owned or had in mind the historic buildings he wanted in place by October, with the exception of the last-minute addition of the Lincoln Courthouse. He had an industrial research complex, a school, a country store, an inn, a livery stable, grist and carding mills, a train station, a joint post office and apothecary, a boarding house and two homes.

However, his center of activity, the village green, had at least two significant gaps — a town hall and a church. For a man with Ford's drive, these presented only minor obstacles. He simply ordered Cutler to design and build the structures right in the village.

Almost simultaneously the two buildings began to rise in August 1929, facing each other at the head and foot of the green. Cutler created a completely original design for the Town Hall (62 and 63), representing the early 1800s Greek Revival style. His chapel design was based on a much larger Universalist church in Bradford, Massachusetts.

The chapel's bricks and doors came from the building in which the Fords were married – the Bryant family home in old Greenfield Township (from which the village name was taken). Ford planned to name the structure the Chapel of Mary-Martha "for his mother and Mrs. Ford's mother," aide William Simonds remembered. "And I think it was the way the story read in the Detroit News. But, anyway, Mrs. Ford sent down word that it was to be the Chapel of Martha-Mary, that her mother was to come first. So the name was changed . . . ."

Clara, with her husband, son Edsel and members of the Roy Bryant family in attendance, broke ground for the chapel early in 1929 (64). Following the original plan, the site was the highest in the village. Young Ford aide Jimmy Humberstone lived, at Ford's request, in the old farmhouse next to the chapel site with his bride (65). Before the house, which predated the village, was torn down, the Humberstones moved into the Sarah Jordan Boarding House. These first two inhabitants of the village soon added a third on May 26, 1929, and named him James Jordan Humberstone.

Chapel construction continued (66) through August. The combined power house and heating plant was built several hundred feet to the rear of the building (67) to keep the chapel's interior (68) free of noise. Ford later ordered five replicas of the Georgian-style chapel constructed in various locations around the country. Only the village building (69) was made of brick.

45

70

71

72

73

Cutler and his crew erected three other buildings before October. The Village Blacksmith Shop (70) and the Armington and Sims Machine Shop (71 and 72) represented typical 19th-century buildings and were furnished with functioning original equipment.

Without a doubt, the last building Ford added before Light's Golden Jubilee was the Tintype Studio (73). As Cutler related:

> The last headache was the day before the celebration. The boss came along and wanted a tintype shop, and we had to have that tintype shop in one day. Didn't we have to beat it? Ebling [Ford photographer] worked his fool head off. I think he got his wife's curtains down there to put on the windows. His wife and mother-in-law fixed up the curtains for the skylight. He was nearly nuts, too, because he had to get the thing operating for the next day. We had to paint the thing and everything to get it in shape, and then it started to rain. It rained all the day of the celebration.

47

Guide

1. Smith's Creek Depot
2. Toll House Cobbler's Shop
3. Plymouth House
4. Post Office
5. Waterford Country Store
6. Gardner House
7. Log House
8. Livery Stable
9. Clinton Inn
10. Village Church
11. Scotch Settlement School
12. Lincoln Court House
13. Town Hall

Guide (Concluded)

Menlo Park
14. Office Building and Library
15. Research Laboratory
16. Carpenter Shed
17. Carbon House
18. Machine Shop
19. Glass House
20. Locomotive Shed
21. Sally Jordan's Boarding House
22. Fort Myers Laboratory
23. Luther Burbank's Office
24. Edison Sub Station
25. Blacksmith Shop
26. Wool Carding Mill
27. Village Machine Shop
28. Grist Mill

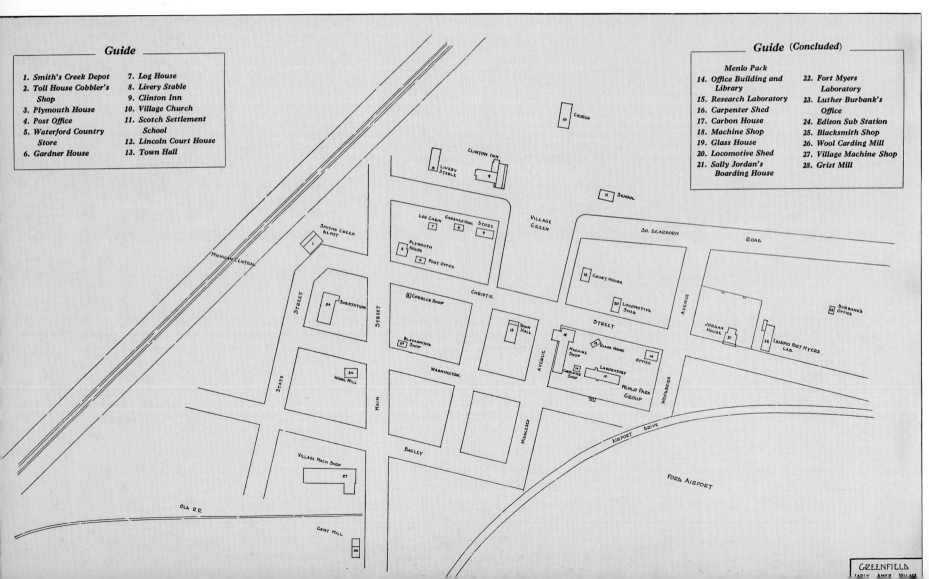

GREENFIELD
EARLY AMER. VILLAGE

74

75

The fever pitch required to turn Ford's dream into a reality of streets and buildings in little more than one year did not escape notice by outsiders. One wrote down his views of the scene in early 1929:

> There is a pattern to the town. You can see that from the car-window. Men and tractors and teams are scraping and preparing its streets [74 and 75]. The clatter of hammers is upon the air. Scaffolding enshrouds buildings, scaffolding is being torn from their completed selves. A gang is laying railroad track straight up to a little depot.

Guests at the October 21 dedication received souvenir maps of the village for the day's touring (76). Resembling only a foundation, number 24 on the map was really an underground Edison substation. (A replica of Detroit's 1886 Edison Illuminating Company building would rise on that spot in 1944.)

Dignitaries sat down to a formal banquet that evening in the museum building (77). Adjacent to the village, this structure had risen from bare ground to magnificence in seven months. The story of that incredible feat began about a year earlier on board an ocean liner in the middle of the Atlantic....

77

49

Independence Hall and an Architect

Henry Ford met Detroit architect Robert O. Derrick on the liner *Majestic* en route to Europe in 1928. Friends of the Edsel Fords, the Derricks were aware that Henry and Clara were on board. On the second day out of port, Ford invited Derrick and his party to tea. During general conversation, Ford asked the architect if he had any suggestions for the design of his proposed museum of Americana. Derrick responded, "Well, I'll tell you, Mr. Ford, the first thing I could think of would be if you could get permission for me to make a copy of Independence Hall in Philadelphia. It is a wonderful building and beautiful architecture and it certainly would be appropriate for a collection of Americana." Ford liked the idea immediately and, once back in Detroit, Derrick obtained the commission.

Unlike most of Ford's assistants during The Edison Institute's formative stages, Derrick was schooled for the job he was performing. After attending Yale and Columbia universities, he joined the New York architectural firm of Murphy and Dana. He opened his own firm in Detroit after World War I and had several major buildings to his credit before accepting the museum design, including the Grosse Pointe Club (1927) and the Hannan Memorial Y.M.C.A. (1927).

Derrick, in his oral reminiscences, related some interesting details about the creation of The Edison Institute (now Henry Ford) Museum:

> I did visit a great many industrial and historical museums and went to Chicago. I remember that I studied the one abroad in Germany [the Deutsches Museum], which is supposed to be one of the best. I had drawings of it. I studied them all very carefully and I did make some very beautiful plans, I thought. Of course, I was going according to museum customs. We had a full basement and a balcony around so the thing wouldn't spread out so far. We had a lot of exhibits to go in the balcony.
>
> I had learned that, in museum practice, you should have a lot more storage space, maintenance space and repair shops than you should have for exhibition. That is why I had the big basement. I didn't even get enough there because I had the floor over it plus the balconies all around. Still, I was short, and I mentioned that to Mr. Ford, but he didn't seem to think it was serious.
>
> He said we would have to have a model made, so we had a model made and it showed the balconies, naturally, and the basement, and he said, "What is this up here?" I said, "That is a balcony for exhibit." He said, "I wouldn't have that; there would be people up there, I could come in and they wouldn't be working. I wouldn't have it." He said, "I have to see everybody." Then he said, "What's this?" I said, "That is the basement down there, which is necessary to maintain these exhibits and to keep things which you want to rotate, etc." He said, "I wouldn't have that; I couldn't see those men down there when I came in. You have to do the whole thing over again and put it on one floor with no balconies and no basements." I said, "Okay," and I went back and we started all over again. What you see now is what we did the second time.

Henry Ford was an elusive man; with so many projects going at once, he almost had to be. Even on as important an undertaking as the museum design, Ford rarely had much time for discussion. "I had an awful time getting anything out of him," Derrick recalled.

> Finally, I had to get almost everything from Mr. [Fred] Black. It got so that I would have to tell Mr. Ford as quickly as I could what was going on. He paid no attention so I went right ahead. I did what I thought was best. That's the way the darn thing got finished.

For the front portion of the museum, Derrick pursued the Independence Hall concept, with replicas of Independence Square's Congress Hall and Old City Hall on the ends.

From my office, we wrote to the city of Philadelphia and asked if they had any measured drawings of Independence Hall. We thought they might have, so that in case of fire or something like that, they could duplicate it. They wrote back that they had measured drawings and would be very glad to show them to us if we would come down there. To send someone down was all right, but it really meant weeks and weeks of study. I told that to Mr. Ford, and I said that it would take a long time and what we ought to have was a copy of those drawings up here, if there is any way to get them. I said, "They won't give them to me." He said, "I'll get them." Within a week, he had the drawings out in Dearborn, so we had them to work with.

In the drawings, which were exact measurements of the existing Independence Hall, there were innumerable mistakes. Pilasters, one over the other, were off center maybe one or two inches and windows were off center, and they weren't at the same height, and sometimes doors were not placed in the center of a wall where they should be. These were hardly

noticeable, maybe two or three inches off. You wouldn't notice it, but we noticed it, so I went to Mr. Ford and said, "I think we ought to make those corrections while we are doing this thing, shouldn't we?" He said, "Oh, no! Make it exactly the same, put in all the mistakes." So, the only place that you can really see where those mistakes are is in the tower. If you look carefully, you will find those big pilasters that go up; then there is sort of a cornice followed by pilasters again and maybe a third one. You will find that they are off center as they go up. They are not in line.

Every interior detail is an exact copy, and the room was kept just exactly as it was with the idea in mind of the purpose it would have to serve. Of course, it couldn't be a Hall of Congress, nor could it be a Supreme Court. We had to take all that furniture out, but the details of the cornices, pilasters, windows, arches and everything are exactly the same as they are in Philadelphia.

78

79

80

Robert O. Derrick's first design for the museum (78, previous page) featured two stories, numerous courtyards and, at the right (where an Education Building was built eight years later), a roundhouse for the additional trains Ford planned to acquire. Ford later rejected the last idea.

Although the front elevation did not change when Ford wanted a one-story version, the rest of the museum did — drastically (79, side elevation of two-story version; 80, revised one-story plan eventually adopted).

A portion of the proposed front corridor (81) included a check room in the left alcove. Furnishings had not yet been determined. The main corridor, stretching into the huge mechanical arts hall in the back of the building, incorporated space along its length for a registration desk, a service office and alcoves for information and first aid. Derrick's main "Exhibition Hall" idea was followed closely (82) with the exception of his suggested use of tile or stone flooring. Ford decided on inlaid teakwood.

81

82

83

On September 27, 1928, minutes after starting the machinery in the newly restored Fort Myers Laboratory in Greenfield Village, Thomas Edison thrust a spade into a hardening concrete block on the site of the planned museum building (83, man to Edison's left believed to be Robert O. Derrick). Luther Burbank once used the spade in his agricultural experiments. Edison's act thus symbolized a key principle Ford wished to illustrate in his historical complex: the union between agriculture and industry in mankind's technological progress. Edison walked off the block, leaving his footprints, then, with Ford at his side, carefully inscribed his signature in front of the spade (84 and 85).

B. R. Brown, construction coordinator on the project, received orders to begin work as soon as possible. "In platting the museum, I found that the concrete was not oriented correctly," Brown recalled. "I was told by Mr. Ford that I couldn't move it, but in order to get the building in the proper location on the site it had to be moved. This was done quite secretly, both lowered and turned, but my guess is that Mr. Ford knew all about it after all."

By April 3, 1929, the museum building was staked out, awaiting construction by the Albert A. Albrecht Company (86). A few unfinished contractor's shacks and, at the right rear, the Ford Airport buildings, stood out. A dirigible mooring mast rose in the distance. Street lamps lined the new Village Road.

86

84

85

87

89

Workers had hoisted roof trusses for the Independence Hall section into place by May 15 (87). In the distance, just to the right of the frame, stood the Sarah Jordan Boarding House and the Fort Myers Laboratory.

Within two months, much of the Independence Hall replica's masonry materialized (88). Frames of the flanking buildings were visible and, at the right, scaffolding marked the location of the rear Exhibition or Mechanical Arts Hall.

On the reverse or courtyard side of the facade, stone and marble quoins (corner pieces) and panels were installed by August 27 (89). This was actually the front side of the Philadelphia building, but both Ford and Derrick wanted the tower to serve as the front entrance. Because the original Independence Hall stood too close to the street, Philadelphians added the tower to the back of the structure (90). Ford wanted the building duplicated as accurately as possible, so he simply turned it around, sacrificing the more decorative side for the tower. Ford closely approximated materials found in the Independence Square buildings, although maintenance factors and modern building codes did demand consideration. Thus, shingle tile of uneven thicknesses approximated the old wood shingles and lead sheeting, painted white, shielded some of the wood surfaces in the clock tower.

88

90

92

91

Workmen laid the floor tiles for a side room off the front entrance lobby in the Independence Hall unit in late August (91). Guests would soon be sitting down to the Light's Golden Jubilee banquet in this room.

Columns were still being erected in the exhibition hall area in early September (92). With a month to go, even the front sections remained far from complete (93).

93

Edsel Ford commissioned a replica of the Liberty Bell for the tower (94). On October 1, workers maneuvered it through the clock aperture (95) after a pulley system hoisted it up from the ground. Once the bell was inside, it was lifted up into the next level. Henry Ford instructed his men not to let the bell peal before President Hoover had first crack at it during the Jubilee.

From the air, the museum building almost seemed to touch old Building 13 of the Engineering Laboratory seven days before the dedication (96). The remains of the old tractor plant still stored the museum's future contents.

With only five days to go, the clock tower appeared complete, while "Old City Hall" and "Congress Hall" at either end received most of the attention (97). The grounds crew worked furiously on the driveways, but they would not finish the lawn by October 21.

The completed entrance to the museum presented a stately appearance a few days after it greeted Light's Golden Jubilee guests (98).

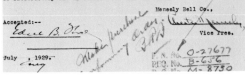

Detroit, Mich., July 29, 1929.

O-2

The Meneely Bell Co. of Troy, N. Y., hereinafter known as The Party of the First Part, hereby agrees to furnish a special bell upon the order of the Ford Motor Co. of Dearborn, Mich., hereinafter known as The Party of the Second Part, as follows:--

Said bell to be a replica of the "Old Liberty Bell" which originally hung in the tower of Independence Hall, Philadelphia, insofar as size, weight and appearance are concerned but is to be correctly proportioned in thickness so as to produce a good tone and be durable.

The same inscription which appears upon the "Old Liberty Bell" and with the same style of letters will be cast upon the bell.

The bell will be made of the finest brands of new Lake Superior copper and new block tin, will be sent subject to trial in tower prior to acceptance or payment and will be guaranteed against fracture or failure of tone for fifteen (15) years.

It is agreed that The Party of the First Part will furnish the bare bell and clapper, only, The Party of the Second Part supplying any mountings or supports that may be decided upon.

It is further understood that the Party of the First Part will cast the bell so that it will appear as did the "Old Liberty Bell" when first made and is not to bear any of the scars or rough spots appearing upon the latter and which were caused by vandals or relic hunters.

The Party of the First Part also agrees to have the bell at Dearborn rail road station on or before October first, nineteen hundred and twenty nine.

The price of the bell is Twenty Eight Hundred Dollars ($2,800), which the Party of the Second Part agrees to pat The Party of the First Part within thirty (30) days after delivery of bell providing the same is satisfactory and in accord with this contract.

Meneely Bell Co.,

Accepted:--

Edsel B. Ford

Vice Pres.,

July , 1929.

F. N. No. O-27677
REQ. No. B-656
M- 8750

94

95

96

98

97

October 21, 1929

This is the only reason Greenfield Village exists – to give us a sense of unity with our people through the generations, and to convey the inspiration of American genius to our youth. As a nation we have not depended so much on rare or occasional genius as on the general resourcefulness of our people. That is our true genius, and I am hoping that Greenfield Village will serve that.

— HENRY FORD

The honor of your presence is requested
by
Mr. Henry Ford and Mr. Edsel Ford
at a
Celebration in honor of
Mr. Thomas Alva Edison
on the occasion of
The Fiftieth Anniversary of his
Invention of the Electric Light
and the dedication of
The Edison Institute of Technology
by
The President of the United States
on Monday, October twenty-first
Nineteen hundred and twenty-nine
Dearborn, Michigan

Chapter Three

Dedication and Jubilee

As to the decorations in the museum building, Mr. Edsel Ford took that matter over. For the outside of the building he engaged Mr. Harry Breitmeyer, a florist in Detroit whom we all knew. He came out there, and they discussed the matter together and decided upon certain greenery, smilax or something similar, to be used in trimming the front of the building.

Well, they'd gotten it almost up, which was the day before the celebration, when Mr. Ford saw it and became pretty much riled up over the fact that these decorations had been put up without his knowing anything about it. He wanted to know who did it. We told him we presumed it was Edsel, with Mr. Breitmeyer.

Mr. Ford ordered it all taken down. Well, shortly after I think Edsel spoke to his father about it, and then Mr. Ford ordered it all put up again!

Ernest G. Liebold, "Reminiscences"

The hectic pace leading up to the October 21 dedication ceremonies accelerated as the day drew near. No one had drawn up a guest list, much less mailed invitations, some four to five weeks before the event. Workmen raced furiously to complete the front portion of the museum where the banquet was to be held. Records indicate there was no time even to photograph the semi-completed museum before the program.

The same frantic tempo governed work in the village. The design, construction, painting and furnishing of the tintype studio, all on October 20, offered a prime example. Details, as Liebold's observations point out, at times seemed all-important to the hosts.

Visiting dignitaries on that rainy October 21 morning saw a muddy, virtually treeless village of about 30 buildings. The front sections of the museum were complete structurally and the banquet rooms inside were finished, although few antiques from Building 13's ever-growing collection had been installed.

The honored guests, Mr. and Mrs. Thomas Edison, traveled to the village on a special train from the Rouge plant station, accompanied by President and Mrs. Herbert Hoover and Henry and Clara Ford. The trip itself, with a wood-burning, c. 1858 locomotive, baggage and passenger cars arriving at Smiths Creek Station, commemorated Edison's work experiences on Michigan's Grand Trunk line some 67 years earlier.

An inspection of completed buildings (including the tintype studio) and in-progress village construction followed. Host Ford could do little about the rain and fog, but he did provide enclosed, horse-drawn carriages to keep the nearly 500 visitors dry between stops. The tour's highlight, of course, was Edison's Menlo Park complex, which was to be the focal point of the evening's Light's Golden Jubilee celebration.

An international radio network, including 140 National Broadcasting Company stations (a record number at that time), broadcast the 7:30 p.m. program honoring Edison. CBS, denied inside access, stationed its announcer outside. The candle-lit dinner began inside the Independence Hall portion of the museum building at 6:15 p.m. Owen D. Young, General Electric board chairman, served as toastmaster. Although host Henry Ford gave no speech, President Hoover and Edison did. After congratulatory telegrams from heads of state were read, messages went out via radio to several different continents.

The real drama, however, waited in the re-created Menlo Park Laboratory. Shortly after dinner, Edison, Hoover and Ford traveled by carriage through kerosene-lit streets to the semi-darkened building. Graham McNamee and Phillips Carlin of NBC described the event to a nation waiting in darkness or in the dim light of candles or gas lamps. The day before, Edison and his former assistant, Francis Jehl, had reconstructed an experimental lamp identical to the one they had made 50 years earlier. Now, on the evening of October 21, 1929, Edison prepared to complete the test, as McNamee described:

October 21, 1929

> But here is Mr. Edison again. While he was at the power house, Mr. Jehl sealed up the old lamp, and it is now ready.... Will it light? Will it burn? Or will it flicker and die, as so many previous lamps had died?
>
> Oh, you could hear a pin drop in this long room.
>
> Now the group is once more about the old vacuum pump. Mr. Edison has the two wires in his hand; now he is reaching up to the old lamp; now he is making the connection.
>
> It lights!

The museum's replica of the Liberty Bell pealed for the first time. Electric lights blinked on across the nation; car horns sounded. The world showed its gratitude to a miraculous invention and its inventor.

None showed appreciation more deeply than Henry Ford. More important than dedicating his beloved village and museum was the opportunity to honor the man who not only had encouraged his first car, but had made possible great advances in industrial technology for the benefit of the entire world.

As Ford's secretary, Liebold, observed:

> We [the Ford Motor Company] got no advertising value or benefit out of it [Light's Golden Jubilee] as far as I know except Mr. Ford was known for what he had done and naturally received that favorable publicity. But it had not been done for that purpose. It was done by Mr. Ford as a sincere appreciation for what Mr. Edison had done for the American people in his development of the electric light.

The Edison Institute had been properly christened. During the next 18 years, Henry Ford would blow enough wind into its sails to give his ship a fascinating educational voyage.

WESTERN UNION

CLASS OF SERVICE
This is a full-rate Telegram or Cablegram unless its character is indicated by a symbol in the check or in the address.

NEWCOMB CARLTON, PRESIDENT   J. C. WILLEVER, FIRST VICE-PRESIDENT

SYMBOLS
BLUE — Day Letter
NITE — Night Message
NL — Night Letter
LCO — Deferred
CLT — Cable Letter
WLT — Week End Letter

The filing time as shown in the date line on full-rate telegrams and day letters, and the time of receipt at destination as shown on all messages, is STANDARD TIME.

Received at Cor. Congress & Shelby Sts., Detroit, Mich. ALWAYS OPEN

Z64 45

CD NEWYORK NY OCT 2 1929 145P

EDSEL FORD

DETROIT MICH

GREATLY APPRECIATE INVITATION OF YOUR FATHER AND YOURSELF
FOR TWENTY FIRST HAD UNFORTUNATELY ALREADY MADE OTHER PLANS
FOR THAT DATE BUT WILL TRY TO REARRANGE KINDLY HAVE YOUR
SECRETARY WRITE ME HOW EARLY IN THE DAY CELEBRATION BEGINS
AND AT WHAT HOUR IT WILL END

JOHN D ROCKEFELLER JR

203P

OCT 4 1929

1a

WESTERN UNION

CLASS OF SERVICE
This is a full-rate Telegram or Cablegram unless its character is indicated by a symbol in the check or in the address.

NEWCOMB CARLTON, PRESIDENT   J. C. WILLEVER, FIRST VICE-PRESIDENT

SYMBOLS
BLUE — Day Letter
NITE — Night Message
NL — Night Letter
LCO — Deferred
CLT — Cable Letter
WLT — Week End Letter

The filing time as shown in the date line on full-rate telegrams and day letters, and the time of receipt at destination as shown on all messages, is STANDARD TIME.

Received at Cor. Congress & Shelby Sts., Detroit, Mich. ALWAYS OPEN

Z25 23

MD NEWYORK NY OCT 4 1929 1045A

EDSEL B FORD

FORD MOTOR CAR CO DETROIT MICH

TELEGRAM RECEIVED HAVE BEEN ABLE TO REARRANGE PLANS AND AM
DELIGHTED TO ACCEPT THE KIND   HOSPITALITY WHICH YOU AND MRS
FORD OFFER ME

JOHN D ROCKEFELLER JR

1113A

OCT 4 1929

1c

POSTAL TELEGRAPH – COMMERCIAL CABLES

CLARENCE H. MACKAY, PRESIDENT

CLASS OF SERVICE DESIRED
DOMESTIC
Telegram
Day Letter
Night Message
Night Letter

CABLE
Full Rate
Deferred
Cable Letter
Week-End Letter

TELEGRAMS TO ALL AMERICA   CABLEGRAMS TO ALL THE WORLD

RECEIVER'S NUMBER
CHECK
TIME FILED
STANDARD TIME

Patrons should check class of service desired; otherwise message will be transmitted as a full-rate communication.

Send the following Telegram, subject to the terms on back hereof, which are hereby agreed to.   Form 2

10.15 AM   Oct 3 1929

Mr John D Rockefeller Jr
26 Broadway
New York City

I hope very much that you will be able to rearrange
your plans so that you can be out here on the twenty
first The events of the day start at approximately
nine o'clock in the morning and finish at about the
same hour in the evening Hope you can come and that
you will be Mrs Ford's and my guest while here A
booklet giving an outline of the program for the day
will be mailed very soon

Edsel Ford

(Personal business)

1b

According to Ernest G. Liebold, who arranged the dedication ceremonies, invitations (see p. 58) to some five hundred world and national dignitaries went out at the last possible moment—probably near the end of September. For such active people, schedule arrangements could pose problems (1, 2, 3 and 4).

Telegram (Ford Motor Company)

BE BRIEF

FR31Z F 31

BV BEVERLYHILLS CALIF 1234P OCT 18 1929

HENRY FORD
    DEARBORN   OCT 18 1929

SURE THANK YOU FOR YOUR INVITATION JUST FOUND WAS ABLE TO
GET AWAY FROM MY PICTURE AND WILL LEAVE BY PLANE IN THE
MORNING HOPE HOOVER MAKES A GOOD SPEECH REGARDS

            WILL ROGERS
                409P

2

Letter to Mr Percival Dodge

October
9th
1929

Mr Percival Dodge
71 Lake Shore Road
Grosse Pointe Mich

Dear Mr Dodge:

        The writer takes the liberty of calling
your attention to the invitation of Mr Henry Ford and
Mr Edsel Ford to attend the Edison Celebration on
October 21st.

        To this you have sent in the acceptance of
yourself and Mrs Dodge.

        To provide for the attendance of the largest
number of persons, we have found it necessary to omit
women from the invitations, except in some unusual circumstances where their presence is necessary by reason
of their friendship or relation to the Edison family.

        Mr Ford hopes therefore to have the privilege
of welcoming you on this ocassion.

                Very truly yours

                E G LIEBOLD

            General Secretary to HENRY FORD

EGL:M

3a

Handwritten acceptance (Marie Curie)

One Fifth Avenue

RECEIVED
OCT -3 1929
Secretary's Office

OCT -3 1929

Madam Marie Curie and
Mrs William Brown Meloney
accept with pleasure the
invitation of Mr Henry Ford
and Mr Edsel Ford to
attend the celebration in
Honor of Mr Thomas A. Edison
on Monday, October twenty-first

    Since Madam Curie is
not strong, Mrs Meloney
is accompanying her at
all functions during her
visit to this country

            Emily J. Hufford
                Secretary

    October first

62   4

The Grosse Pointe School

The Grosse Pointe School

GROSSE POINTE FARMS, MICHIGAN

FORREST B. WING, HEADMASTER

Oct. 14, 1929

OCT 15 1929 RECEIVED
OCT 15 1
OCT r 19

Mr. E. G. Liebold,
Gen. Secretary to Henry Ford,
Dearborn, Mich.

Dear Mr. Liebold:

        Pardon the error. I unintentionally
took it for granted that we were both invited. We
both understand clearly the reasons for limiting the
attendance.

        I shall be delighted to attend the
Edison Celebration in person.

                Very truly yours,

                Percival Dodge,

3b

5

6

The Edisons arrived in Dearborn a few days before the
dedication ceremonies to familiarize themselves with the village
and museum. Accompanied by the Fords, they inspected the
Menlo Park restorations (5). After a tour of the laboratory,
Edison said, "Ford, it's 99.9 percent perfect." Ford, pleased,
but obviously curious about any inaccuracies in the meticulous
work, asked the aged inventor what he had missed. "Oh,"
answered Edison, "our floor was never as clean as this."

On October 20, Edison and his former assistant, Francis
Jehl, prepared cotton thread filaments (6) for the reenactment
lamp (7).

After the work, while reminiscing about Menlo Park
experiences, Edison pointed out the window toward the home
of the compound's carpenter in the 1870s. He had momentarily
forgotten he was in Dearborn, not New Jersey. Henry Ford,
Ed Cutler and crew had done their homework.

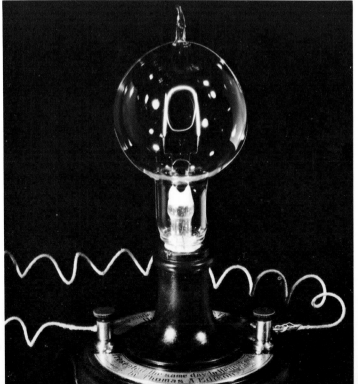

7

63

Operating Schedule

October 21, 1929
(prepared by Ernest G. Liebold)

Movement of Ford Special Train
Rouge Plant Yard to Dearborn

10:00 A.M.	Arrive Dearborn.
KLEBBA:	Arrange to have Ford Tudor Sedan bearing "Special" label with driver and attendant. Secure President's hand baggage from his valet Boris for transfer to Mr. Ford's residence. Car to remain at Residence for orders.
BENNETT:	Provide proper Escort, if necessary, to enable car to proceed through traffic without interruption.
12:45	Return of President to Mr. Ford's residence for lunch. Arrangements should be made to direct cars bearing "Guests" to Celebration in above party to East Gate at Greenfield for lunch at Clinton Inn, if desired, or to convey parties to other points desired.

President's Visit to Ford Rouge Plant, Greenfield
and return to Residence

2:00 P.M.	Party Scheduled to leave Ford Residence.
KLEBBA:	Number of cars required will be ascertained and furnished later.
BENNETT:	Please arrange Escort and protection in co-operation with Secret Service along following route, Ford Residence to Michigan, Michigan to Coolidge, Coolidge to Ford Plant and from Ford Plant to Coolidge Highway to Butler Road, west to Division Road to Airport Drive to Southfield Road to East Gate on Airport Drive and into Village, South Dearborn Road Gate.
3:45 P.M.	Arrival at Greenfield.
4:00 P.M.	Party will be supervised by U.S. Secret Service in co-operation with our own service where necessary in Village Grounds.
KLEBBA:	Necessary cars should be held available for President's return to Mr. Ford's Residence about 5:15 P.M. or when required. Remainder of party will return to Special Train on Experi-

mental Laboratory siding at Power House.

Arrange for cars necessary to convey members of Party to train and from train to Independence Hall at 6:05 P.M. Secret Service to be transported by their own cars according to their instructions.

BENNETT:	Provide Escort and protection in co-operation with Secret Service from Greenfield at 5:15 P.M. or thereabouts to Ford Residence.

Trip from Residence to Independence Hall
and to President's Special Train

6:30 P.M.	Arrive Independence Hall.
KLEBBA:	Provide all cars necessary for Secret Service and others.
BENNETT:	Provide Escort and necessary additional protection in co-operation with Secret Service from Residence to Independence Hall. Same Route as previous to East Gate on Airport Drive to Hall.
KLEBBA:	Send to Residence for President's baggage at 7:00 P.M. and deliver to Boris, President's valet on special train parked at Ford Experimental Laboratory.
7:40 P.M.	President, Mr. Edison, Mr. Ford and party leave for Menlo Park Laboratory.
8:10 P.M.	Party returns to Independence Hall.
8:45 to 9:00 P.M.	President will leave with Mr. Ford and Mr. Edison for Private Car.
KLEBBA:	Arrange all cars outside Independence Hall to convey Party when required.
BENNETT:	Provide Escort and protection from Independence Hall through our own private roads to President's Special train parked adjacent to Power House at Experimental Laboratory.

At 10 a.m., on schedule, the 1860s Sam Hill wood-burning locomotive (renamed the President for the occasion) puffed its way through the rainy gloom on a special spur to the Smiths Creek Station platform (8). The engine had been reconditioned at the Ford Rouge plant locomotive shop. It pulled two passenger cars, constructed earlier in the year at the Rouge plant, and a baggage car, which was a replica of the one Thomas Edison worked in and burned as a boy. An October 12 photograph (9) shows the train, at left, pulling up to Smiths Creek Station in a trial run before the dedication. A little farther down the line sits the long train shed built to shelter it. Twin Michigan Central Railroad tracks parallel the village spur. Michigan Avenue winds along the Rouge River banks.

The peculiar-looking engine on the other set of tracks (8) also performed during dedication festivities. This beautifully crafted replica of the 1829 English Rocket had been built, at Ford's request, by Robert Stephenson & Co. of Darlington, England. The Stephenson firm had also built the original, which won field trials at Rainhill, England, in October 1829, thus earning the claim of the first successful railroad locomotive. Although Ford did not ride in it on October 21, he had driven it earlier, as he had the President on numerous occasions.

8

9

Despite the rain, a crowd gathered to welcome the Edisons, Hoovers and Fords (10). Irving Bacon, assigned to photograph the event as he had the cornerstone ceremony the year before, waited in the crowd. Getting to the platform had not been easy, however. After taking pictures and movies at the Rouge plant station, "Krausmann [his assistant] and I, wearing raincoats, jumped in our car and highballed it out to the village to get there before the train would arrive," Bacon recalled.

> Instead of going through the gate, we parked our car on Michigan Avenue, opposite the Smiths Creek Station. Grabbing our cameras, tripods and small stepladder, we dashed across the railroad tracks and climbed over the fence as secret service men shouted and ran to stop us. But we were over before you could say Jack Robinson. It is a wonder that they didn't shoot us. At that, we were there just in time. My little stepladder came in very handy. Standing on it, I could shoot the pictures over the heads of the crowd.

10

President Hoover assisted Edison down the steps from the baggage car replica and into the waiting throngs (11), where they were joined by their wives and the Fords.

Because of the rainy, muddy conditions in the village, the hosts provided horse-drawn and, for the most part, covered carriages and cabs (12). Guests certainly appreciated Ford's volume collecting that day!

After leaving the station, the carriages transported passengers to various stops in the village, including the Sarah Jordan Boarding House (13). Employees dressed in period costumes contributed to the atmosphere.

The presidential party lunched at the Fords' Fair Lane estate. Other guests ate at the stately Clinton Inn. Groundsmen had rolled the village green lawn into place only the day before.

11

12

During the afternoon, guests roamed freely through the village. Hoover and Edison lit symbolic fires in, respectively, the Lincoln Courthouse fireplace and the Menlo Park Machine Shop boiler. The President's act honored government and home while the inventor's recognized science and industry.

As the day's activities drew to a close, special cars transported guests to their hotels in time to prepare for the evening banquet. Ford's hard-working staff must have experienced quite a letdown. As aide William Simonds summed up, "Those of us who had assisted during the day in explaining the history of the building to the guests were soaked to the skin."

Simonds evidently dried off in sufficient time to attend the banquet. He noted:

> As one stepped into the lobby of the museum that evening from the drenching outdoors, it was as if one had entered fairyland. All was candle-lit. Figures great in contemporary history filed up the broad winding staircase to leave their wraps, then descended to an array of glittering tables that stretched to the right under the brilliant candelabra to the speakers' table.

67

13

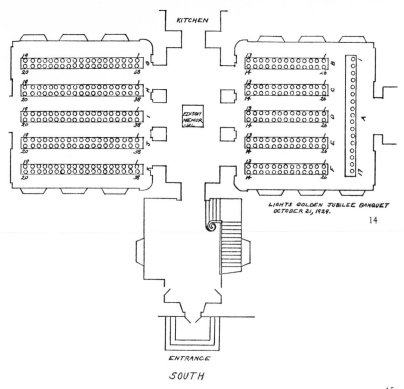

NORTH

KITCHEN

EDISON
MEMOR
IAL

LIGHTS GOLDEN JUBILEE BANQUET
OCTOBER 21, 1929.

14

ENTRANCE

SOUTH

15

ROBERT HUTTON & CO.

622 FORT STREET EAST

DETROIT, MICH. October 23, 1929

SOLD TO _____ Ford Motor Car Co.

ORDER NO. _____ Mr. Griffith

INVOICE NO. 7838 _____ Dearborn, Michigan.

E B Ford Order No. 2457

Installing stove hoods in Independence Hall			
at Ford Museum Group.			
733 lbs Galvanised Iron	@ .063	46.18	
118 hrs Tinner	1.10	129.80	
50 hrs " Helper	.65	32.50	
80% Overhead on Labor		129.84	
		338.32	
10% profit		33.83	
		$372.15	

68

Guests were to sit on either side of the entrance arcade (14). Behind the scenes, the central corridor was lined with warming ovens and other kitchen accessories needed by the caterer, Detroit's Book-Cadillac Hotel. Details, as on all great occasions, seemed nearly endless, as sample paperwork attested (15).

Candles, hand-dipped in the village (signaling the start of the complex's crafts program), provided almost all of the banquet's lighting. Ford would permit no electric lights until Edison successfully reenacted his experiment and threw a main switch in Menlo Park. Problems complicated the plan. B. R. Brown, the man who had secretly moved the cornerstone, was again in the middle:

> The life of a tallow candle is very short. We time-checked all the wax candles that we could get our hands on to see if we could give him [Ford] what he wished. It developed that none of them would burn long enough, besides dripping on the tables. I had been instructed not to have an electric light in the place, but . . . we assembled about four or five flood lights back of the palms and out of sight. They came in handy when the banquet was over! As the candles went out, we switched the lights on. Nothing was ever said later about the use of these lights. I guess they were just taken for granted and accepted.

Ernest Liebold recalled only one mishap.

> When the President came in, I was to give a signal to Mr. Lovett and the orchestra, and they were to play "Hail to the Chief." I was waving at them, but I believe the Secret Service men thought I was going to hit Hoover over the head or something! They gave me an awful stare. I couldn't get the music. Finally I had enough sense to run out to the broadcasting room and found that they had failed to turn on the switch for the amplifiers! The radio people were responsible for that.

An Animated "Who's Who"

After a reception on the museum's second floor, guests at the dedication banquet took their seats downstairs and dinner was served. During the meal, NBC began its international broadcast of the ceremonies:

> Good evening, ladies and gentlemen of the radio audience. This is Graham McNamee speaking from Dearborn, Michigan, where Henry Ford and Edsel Ford are entertaining one of the most notable gatherings assembled in the annals of American history to honor Thomas Alva Edison on the occasion of the Fiftieth Anniversary of his invention of the first practical incandescent lamp . . . .
>
> I have attended many celebrations, but I cannot recall ever attempting to describe one staged in a more perfect setting.
>
> The dinner that is now going on is taking place in one of the buildings of The Edison Institute of Technology. This building is an exact reproduction of Independence Hall in Philadelphia. I have just been thinking that the world could not celebrate its emancipation from darkness more fittingly than in this building, which is associated in the minds of all of us with freedom and progress . . . .
>
> Against this background, imagine the chequered effect of black and white evening dress, the brilliant splashes of color provided by the uniforms of military attachés and the great stylists of Paris and Fifth Avenue.
>
> I had some idea before I started this broadcast of trying to tell you who was here tonight, but really, I do not know where to start. It seems as if everybody I ever heard of is here; a good deal of an animated *Who's Who* . . . .
>
> Yes, here is one that will interest you — Madame Curie. You know who she is, of course — the woman co-discoverer of radium. You would not think to look at this quiet Polish woman, that she upset the ideas of the whole scientific world on the structure of matter.
>
> And beyond her I see one of the electrical leaders of Japan, H. Haro.
>
> And let me see — yes — here is Orville Wright, who with his brother Wilbur invented the airplane.
>
> There is Will Rogers, John D. Rockefeller, Jr., M. S. Sloane and A. W. Robertson.
>
> I could go on indefinitely telling you who is here, but there is not time. You just have to imagine all of the people you read about in the daily newspapers come to life and gathered in one place for one purpose.

Ford did not permit flash cameras because of their disruptive smoke. Thus, no visual documentation of the banquet exists other than the painting by Ford staff artist and photographer, Irving Bacon (see p. 73).

The NBC microphone used for the Jubilee broadcast (16) later assumed an honored place in the museum collections.

Hoover, Edison and Ford left after dinner for Menlo Park where Edison reenacted his successful lighting of the incandescent lamp 50 years earlier. Moments after he connected the wires, making the cotton thread filament glow from red to startling white light (17, left to right: Francis Jehl, Hoover, Edison, Ford), he threw a switch and the entire Menlo Park complex and museum building were bathed in light (18, the lab lit during a dress rehearsal). Simultaneously, bells pealed and radio listeners across the globe turned on the electric lights in their homes, stores and automobiles.

Speech-making awaited in the banquet room. Master of Ceremonies Owen D. Young saluted not only Edison, but the distinguished crowd that had gathered to honor him.

> Most conspicuous of the men, is our host, Mr. Henry Ford. He has built The Edison Institute of Technology, and this industrial museum in your honor. Other men could have built an institute, but Mr. Ford has done something more.
>   When certain materials are exposed to radium—and no greater honor could be done to Mr. Edison and to this company than to have the presence of Madame Curie—(Applause)—when certain materials, as I said, are exposed to radium, the glow of that marvelous element continues for time and perhaps eternity. It lights your dark places like the radium exposed hands on our watches, and so Mr. Ford has brought to Greenfield Village not only every piece of apparatus which Mr. Edison used at Menlo Park, but every chair, brick and stone and even earth, in order that these common things, once exposed to elevating the personality of Thomas A. Edison, may radiate from this museum for generations to come, the vitality of which is his. (Applause)

Edison, deeply moved by the entire tribute, brought his emotions under control and spoke briefly. In concluding, he said, "As to Henry Ford, words are inadequate to express my feelings. I can only say to you that, in the fullest and richest meaning of the term—he is my friend."

The Edison Institute (19, early logo), Ford's dream of many years, was now a reality. Hosts and participants rated October 21 a great success (20). Only the formal filing of incorporation papers remained in a year that had seen tremendous progress for the preservation of America's past (21). Three trustees and members of the association were named: Henry Ford, president; Clara J. Ford, vice-president; and Edsel B. Ford, secretary-treasurer.

18

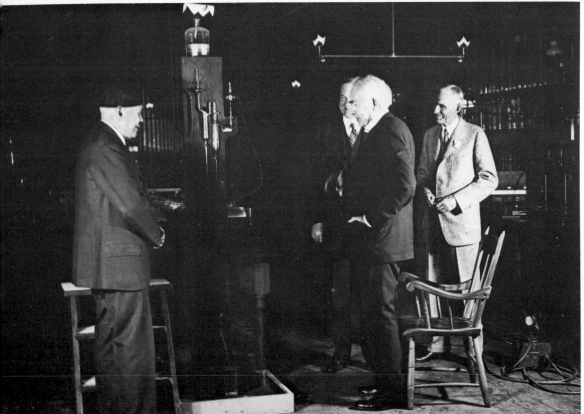

17

Westinghouse Electric & Manufacturing Company

Room 1923 Grant Building
310 Grant Street.
Pittsburgh, Pa.

Office of
A.W.Robertson
Chairman

October 24, 1929.

Mr. Henry Ford,
Dearborn, Michigan.

Dear Mr. Ford:

I enjoyed my visit at Dearborn and Greenfield Village as much as any experience I have ever had. I hope that you and your son are happy over the great success of this undertaking. One thing that I have promised myself is that my three children, now between the ages of eight and twelve, must spend a day sometime looking over this Village.

This letter would not be complete if I did not mention the fact that when I offered to pay my hotel bill, I found that my money was not wanted as the bill had been charged to you, and I thank you for that additional courtesy.

With all good wishes for your continued good health and happiness, I am,

Yours very truly,

A W Robertson

A. W. ROBERTSON.

20

UNITED STATES OF AMERICA

The State of Michigan

DEPARTMENT OF STATE

TO ALL TO WHOM THESE PRESENTS SHALL COME:

I, John S. Haggerty, Secretary of State of the State of Michigan and Custodian of the Great Seal thereof, Do Hereby Certify that Articles of Association of

THE EDISON INSTITUTE

were duly filed in this office on the 23rd day of December A.D., Nineteen Hundred and Twenty nine and the said Company is authorized to commence its business in conformity with Act 84, Public Acts of 1921, as amended.

In Testimony Whereof, I have hereunto set my hand and affixed the Great Seal of the State at the Capitol in the City of Lansing, this Twenty-third day of December A.D. 1929.

John S. Haggerty
Secretary of State

FORM NO. 506 4-2-29 4M

21

71

19

An Artist Remembers

Probably Henry Ford's only regret in later years concerning the dedication and Light's Golden Jubilee ceremonies was the disturbing fact that no photographs preserved the memory of the occasion. To compensate somewhat for this void, in the mid-1930s he instructed his staff artist, Irving Bacon, to paint a huge (17 feet by 7 feet) canvas of the banquet. Bacon started at once, working in his Engineering Laboratory studio. His oral reminiscences recalled the involved procedures:

> Mr. Liebold dug up the blueprints of table arrangements, the numbers on the tables and the seats allotted to the guests. The first thing I asked for was to have letters sent out for photographs of those who attended and also to ask them to tell who sat near or beside them. This proved to be the most important piece of work I ever did for him, or anyone else, in fact. When it was finally completed, it showed 266 recognizable portraits.
>
> In the composition, I took liberties to help make the picture present the guests in natural poses as they sat listening to Thomas Edison making his brief speech before the microphones at the speaker's tables.
>
> In order to show as many persons as possible, I composed the scene to cover an angle of 120 degrees in width with a standpoint a trifle behind the speakers' table, with a platform supplying the necessary elevation. The horizon was six feet high. To get in as many celebrities and the Boss's friends as possible, I left out the secret service men and others present who were not on the invitation list. Because of the angles of the photographs I had to work from, I was forced to switch the guests about. In checking positions at the speakers' table, I found that Mrs. Ford was listed as sitting at the left side. There I drew her in the background. She later emphatically insisted that she sat on the right side in the foreground, so her position was changed. In general, I made the picture as authentic as I could to get the best results.
>
> First, to get the proper perspective, I made a tiny projection from the blueprint of the table arrangements. This was enlarged to 15 inches wide, then 3 feet, and finally to a 6-foot cartoon, on which I carefully drew in all the characters.
>
> A lot of research work was necessary. The Book-Cadillac Hotel had put on the banquet, furnishing the tables, golden chairs, silver, dishes, linen, candelabras and golden table runners. Their headwaiter had been present. He gave me samples of the dishes, cutlery and two chairs, in addition to letting me make a sketch of him. This I used in the foreground. Our librarian searched books, magazines and newspapers, hunting for pictures of guests.
>
> Several studies were made of background sections of the scene of the banquet. For the figures in the foreground, I made charcoal drawings from models in evening costume and then oil studies to get the color. To attain the correct perspective on the big canvas, I used a chalk line with a vanishing point 100 feet away to the right.

During his years of work (the painting was completed in 1945), Bacon received help from Ford staffers and Ford family members, including the suggestion to add standing figures along the sides and back. This allowed Bacon to include many more people. The artist recalled Henry Ford's asking him to

> "Put Edsel and my daughter-in-law Eleanor, also young Henry and Benson, my grandsons, in the picture. They couldn't be at the party because they were ill and were quarantined. This is our picture, and they should, by all means, be in there. It's going to make a great painting."
>
> This, of course, called for more research.
>
> Thomas Edison's grandson, Edison Sloane, was with his parents the night of the banquet. He and the Ford boys were all placed together in the lower right-hand corner of the picture. Adding them helped the composition greatly and made it far more interesting. It seemed incomplete without the Edsel Ford family.

Clara Ford offered her opinion as well: "'I had no idea it was so large,' she said. 'Mr. Bacon, you have made Mr. Edison appear too young. He should look much older. The color on Mr. Ford's face should be paler. Now Edsel is very good, but the light under his eyes should be subdued.'"

Bacon provided a numbered key to the notables in the painting, creating a unique, if not totally accurate, record of the event.

(22) *Bacon sketching in his Engineering Lab studio.*

(23) *The completed painting.*

1930-1947

It is to be an institution of learning for young fellows and old fellows, for everybody who wants to know the greatness of our country and what has made it great.

— HENRY FORD

Chapter Four

The Complex Comes to Life

"Well, Mr. Ford, there are a lot of interesting ideas in these exhibits you've got down in the museum, because I've seen some of them. Why don't you hurry up and get the museum opened so we engineers can go down there and spend some time roaming through there?"

His reply was something like this: "Oh, no, I don't want to hurry up and get that done. If I get that done, I'll never have anything to do on this earth. When you don't have anything to do, then you're ready to die."

Harold Hicks, "Reminiscences"

This exchange with a workman about a year after the 1929 dedication indicates at least one thing about Henry Ford and his village and museum: he was in no hurry to open them to the public.

The Edison Institute's original purpose was educational. The village and museum exhibits were to provide hands-on study aids for students. The stated goals of the non-profit corporation, listed in the Articles of Association filed with the state of Michigan on December 23, 1929, were:

(a) To assemble and exhibit, publish and disseminate historical, scientific, sociological and artistic information and to do any and all things calculated directly or indirectly to advance the cause of education, whether general, technical, sociological or aesthetic.

(b) To demonstrate, for educational purposes, the development of American arts, sciences, customs and institutions by reproducing or re-enacting the conditions and circumstances of such development in any manner calculated to convey a realistic picture thereof.

The official corporate name was The Edison Institute. Greenfield — The Early-American Village gradually became known as Greenfield Village. First called The Industrial Museum, the museum later became The Edison Institute Museum. The second title continued in use until several years after Ford's death in 1947, when it was officially changed to The Henry Ford Museum. The public, of course, would continue to refer to it for some time variously as The Ford Museum, Ford's Early American Village, The Dearborn Museum, Henry Ford Pioneer and Historical Museum and, somewhat less reverently, Mr. Ford's Doll's-House.

As the number of people requesting tours through the expanding village grew from about 400 a day in 1929 to nearly 1,000 a day by 1933 (some were admitted, many were turned away), Ford agreed to open the doors officially. A visitors' gatehouse was completed in May, and on June 22, 1933, the public was admitted.

Initially patrons paid 25¢ each for village and museum admission. Children entered for 10¢ and school groups were admitted free. Attendance for both facilities numbered 148,741 for the remaining months of 1933. By 1934, the total had climbed to 247,748. Ford made no real effort to profit from admissions or sale of souvenir postcards and such craft items as stone-ground flour, hand-woven textiles and tintypes. In fact, in the first years, each visitor cost the institute about $5.

Institute officials were unconcerned about increasing attendance figures. 1930s public relations and guide manager William A. Simonds noted: "Mr. Ford said more than once he didn't want to make any money out of the project, so we weren't worried about that end of it." The crowds, in fact, surprised them, and the staff had to hustle to stay one step ahead of the problems created.

1930-1947

At the outset, visitors boarded horse-drawn carriages at the new village gatehouse for transport to the Clinton Inn's welcoming center. Lines of people, stacked four abreast outside the gatehouse, however, forced discontinuation of this service. Fears of overworking the village horses prevented the introduction of paid rides. Thus, to maintain the 18th- and 19th-century atmosphere, horse-drawn vehicles simply rumbled along empty or, on occasion, carried special visitors.

Curiosity was not the only appetite whetted on a trip to the village and museum. With displays exhibited over a 260-acre area, it was (and certainly still is today) difficult for most visitors to view as much as desired without feeling hunger pains. The first pre-1933 food service consisted of hamburgers from the 1890s "Owl" Night Lunch Wagon, one of the haunts from his Detroit youth that Henry Ford transplanted to the village. Clinton Inn luncheon service started and stopped rather abruptly — possibly because it interfered with village schoolchildren eating there. The 1931 opening of Henry Ford's airport hotel, The Dearborn Inn, a few hundred yards from the village, eased the institute's food problems before big crowds began attending.

According to Ford's wishes, both the village and museum stayed open seven days a week, year-round, until the United States entered World War II. However, a number of village buildings remained closed to the public. Either they were structurally or decoratively incomplete, the schools were using them or Ford simply feared possible damage by uncaring people.

Visitors initially did not wander around on their own. Guides covered certain zones, staying with a group for a specified number of buildings. This sytem eventually gave way to one assigning guides to specific structures.

When the first buildings were going up in the village, Henry Ford or one of his assistants would escort guests to points of interest. After the dedication, however, Ford aides began recruiting village and museum guides from the ranks of the Henry Ford Trade School. This practice became a full-fledged program after 1933, supplemented by area high school students. During the summer months the young guide staff could reach 150. Older village schoolgirls took on guide work in the later years, although both Henry and Clara Ford resisted this. "One reason that made it necessary to be careful was that the girls were young, many of them," Simonds noted, "and of course the guides were young fellows, too, and I know it was for one thing Mrs. Ford's idea that we should not let them get to be too familiar with each other."

One young aide, Charles R. Smith, Jr., related his experience:

> On February 4, 1934, I reported to William A. Simonds for work in Greenfield Village as a guide. That spring Mr. Simonds asked that all new guides put in a day on the Ford farms, and I believe this went on for several months. We were to be paid in tomatoes.
>
> I was first stationed in the museum where, although the teak floor wasn't even laid, we took visitors around in groups. There were many crated and disassembled machines outside the building in an adjacent field awaiting their turn to be brought in, put in working order and cleaned up.
>
> After my initial guide work in the museum, I was stationed in the village at various points from time to time, mainly in the post office to carding mill area. Although we saw Mr. Ford's car driving around the village back roads nearly every day, it wasn't very often that he would stop in my sections; he was principally interested in the new buildings being set up, i.e., those he had recently acquired and which were being reconstructed in the village.

1930-1947

When Ford did stop, he often created problems. People would flock around him, a situation not to his liking. Eventually, the guide staff received instruction in methods to keep the public away from him.

Ford appeared in the museum only when he had a specific purpose. He probably had reasons for many years since museum construction extended well into the 1930s. While workers had finished the interior by 1940, an observer noted it would take "several years more to complete the exhibits."

In the village, the automaker sought a change of pace from company pressures. He indulged in three favorite activities while there: tinkering with machinery and watchmaking tools in various buildings; visiting with Greenfield Village schoolchildren; and inspecting construction work. Building continued constantly, especially before World War II, the peak growth period for the village. By 1940, the 1929 collection of 30 buildings had grown to 68. Another 20 were added before Ford's death in 1947, an average of three to four new structures each year.

In all areas the driving force and only true management came from Henry Ford himself. While aides preferred to arrange village buildings chronologically, Ford grouped the buildings in related clusters. In the museum, little progress in organization and classification could come during his lifetime. Both facilities grew solely from his ideas. Thus, he avoided employment of museum professionals who might make changes.

The growing number of children enrolled in Ford's Greenfield Village school system made full use of the educational and historical resources. Beginning with 32 pupils in the 1929 Scotch Settlement School class, the schools soon expanded into seven historic buildings, the museum itself and, in 1937, a new recreation and education building. At the system's peak, students in kindergarten through post-high school technical levels numbered almost 300.

The educational experience involved a unique mixture of traditional one-room school techniques, modern methods, practical experience and even occasional field trips with "Mr. Ford." Ford was determined that his students would learn practical skills so that their transfer from school to the working world would be less abrupt. Not all was hard work, however. Ford allowed his charges the run of the village and museum — often to the dismay of employees. Guides were instructed to keep the public distant from the schoolchildren. Ford at times even encouraged pranks. In any case, the schools and education came first in his directives.

One high school student addressed Ford's theory of practical education, well known to most of them, in a 1940 issue of *The Herald,* the weekly school newspaper:

> The philosophy that one "learns by doing" is well shown in the Village schools in the application of textbook theory to practical problems in the machine shop, for instance; in the planting and tending of small gardens; and in the homemaking practiced in the Secretary House and the Webster House.
> Each year sees the expansion of this flexible system to meet new needs that may arise; yet the fundamental precepts as taught from the McGuffey *Readers* are basic to all developments.

Henry Ford operated schools in many states and nations, at one time hoping to have a million students enrolled in his system. Often of the one-room variety, some schools, such as the Henry Ford Institute of Agricultural Engineering near Chelmsford, England, featured experimental and vocational training.

A system of ten Ford-managed rural schools in Michigan joined The Edison Institute system during the 1930s. Other Ford-run schools operated in Georgia, Massachusetts (at the Wayside Inn property), Michigan's Upper Peninsula (near Ford timber operations) and Brazil (for his rubber plantation workers' children). The Henry Ford Trade School offered instruction to young men at various Detroit manufacturing plants and eventually Greenfield Village. One of the first and the longest-running of Ford's schools, the Henry Ford Trade School (1916-52) evolved from Ford's Dearborn Valley Farm School (1911-16) for orphan boys.

Thomas Edison died in 1931, only two years after Ford dedicated The Edison Institute in his name. Henry Ford carried on the educational inspiration Edison had given him in 1896 by personally guaranteeing preservation of the artifacts and ideals that built America. Two great tragedies pulled him away from his beloved village and museum: war, which he had actively opposed throughout his life, and the death of his only son, Edsel, in 1943.

Reassuming the presidency of the Ford Motor Company after Edsel's death, Henry found less time to spend with the physical objects of man's progress that meant so much to him. He also found less time to devote to the young people that he liked to call his "endowment" for The Edison Institute.

After suffering a mild stroke in 1945, Ford passed the Ford Motor Company's reins to his grandson, Henry Ford II. Though he still sought the peace of the past he had re-created, he remained more a spectator than a leader at the institute. Village and museum operations were thrown into limbo from 1945 until his passing at age 83 in April 1947. After Ford's illness in 1945, his chief architect and village planner, Ed Cutler, wrote: "What will become of the village and us is anybody's guess, but I do know our expansion program is halted for the present." An unsure path lay ahead for the institute Henry Ford had created and nurtured.

1930-1947

Dedication excitement was still in the air when workmen resumed construction of the museum's huge eight-acre exhibition hall. By November 6, 1929, more of the skylight beams were in place (1). Within two months, much of the structural work, including the 180 support columns, was complete. The back roof was on and glass window / ventilation panels were installed by 1930. Inside, painters finished the huge expanses of ceiling (2), and although the teakwood floor would not be finished until 1938 (concrete blocks were used temporarily), the unique column radiators were already evident.

Ford's English agent, Herbert F. Morton, acquired some priceless early engines in England. After dismantling them, he traveled to Dearborn to oversee their installation. Some were so large they had to be anchored below ground level (3), with necessary excavation work taking place after the roof was on the museum.

The Edison Institute Museum looked resplendent in contrast to its neighbors by November 1931 (4). Only stacks of lumber remained of the old tractor plant and Building 13 behind the museum. The antiques by this time had found a new home next door. The Dearborn Inn, built that year as one of the world's first airport hotels, appears at the upper right of the photograph.

6

5

80

9

Village construction, too, picked up after the dedication ceremonies. Ed Cutler set up his office in the Plymouth House and plunged into work. One of his first projects (several would proceed simultaneously) undoubtedly involved reconstructing the 1750 Secretary Pearson House from Exeter, New Hampshire (5, c. 1929). Although Cutler found the house with numerous later additions at the back, he restored it as nearly as possible to what he believed to be its earlier condition. This included a secret staircase leading to the attic. The house stood near the far end of South Dearborn Road by the summer of 1930 (6, c. 1934). In May 1932, the museum served as a staging area for trial room arrangements of the Secretary House furnishings (7, with museum collection items showing through a "window").

One of Cutler's next jobs contrasted sharply with the stately Secretary House. Charles Proteus Steinmetz had built a summer cabin on the banks of Viele Creek, a tributary of the Mohawk River near Schenectady, New York, in 1896. The electrical wizard spent his summers there, usually in solitary study, but sometimes with friends and associates (8, summer 1919, Steinmetz at left as the man in the middle actually takes the picture by pulling a string rigged to the camera's shutter). Lightning had struck the little building before it was presented to Henry Ford in 1930 (9). Ford left it in its rustic condition when he moved it to the banks above the Rouge River in the village.

10

11

In June 1930 a small, rather nondescript frame house was erected on South Dearborn Road (10). Located in the area presently occupied by the Swiss watchmaker's chalet, the 1868 Clark House from rural Wayne County, Michigan, suffered the unusual fate of being torn down in later years. Evidently Ford felt the house contributed little to the village.

The whole village idea was one of flowing change. Buildings were moved and removed, ideas were initiated and just as quickly terminated. Behind the houses along the east side of South Dearborn Road, in an area commonly termed the flats, Ford at different times intended to establish a bird sanctuary in honor of his friend, naturalist John Burroughs, or a Seminole Indian village. Another early plan sought to have people live and work in the village, performing traditional tasks and crafts. Although a few, such as Sarah Jordan Boarding House residents, the Humberstones, and Smiths Creek Depot inhabitant, W. W. Taylor, did serve as living "exhibits," the idea proved impractical and Ford discontinued it. He did retain working craftspeople during the day, however.

Soon after the dedication, a group of buildings reflecting America's ancestral European life arrived in the village from the Cotswold Hills area of southern England. Henry Ford had instructed his English agent, Herbert Morton, to find a typical Cotswold stone house for Greenfield Village. Morton eventually located the c. 1620 Rose Cottage in Chedworth, Gloucestershire (11), and discovered to his great delight that it was for sale. After he purchased it for "Mr. Ford," Morton hired a builder and expert on Cotswold architecture to restore the house in England. Attaining an appearance more reflective of the 17th century required some fairly major alterations. Morton's men went to work on the house and barn (12, the barn at right, without chimneys).

After completing the changes, Morton's men dismantled the cottage and barn and packed them with gravel in strong sacks for shipment to Dearborn. A few of the English builders came

12

Mr Frank Campsall
Personal Secretary to Mr Henry Ford
DEARBORN
Michigan
U S A

7 Oct 1929
IN YOUR REPLY PLEASE QUOTE
DEPARTMENT

Dear Mr Campsall;

ALL STATEMENTS OR AGREEMENTS CONTAINED IN THIS LETTER ARE CONTINGENT ON STRIKES, ACCIDENTS, FIRES, OR ANY OTHER CAUSES BEYOND OUR CONTROL AND ALL CONTRACTS ARE SUBJECT TO APPROVAL BY THE SIGNATURE OF A DULY AUTHORIZED EXECUTIVE OFFICER OF THIS COMPANY. CLERICAL ERRORS SUBJECT TO CORRECTION.

The modifications to the Cotswold Cottage at Chedworth are now complete, and enclosed are a number of photographs showing the building in its present shape.

The added features are the Porch, Dormer Window and the Bay Window to the No.1 section, and the Door Head to the No.2 section, and every window in the cottage is now equipped with old Iron Casements and Leaded Lights.

These Casements and the glass used therein are genuine old pieces found in local jobbing builders' yards, cut and altered to suit our requirements.

In the present building the ceilings are fully plastered and the joists hidden, but during re-erection, the ceiling can be plastered between the joists and thus the original features of the old brown and white ceiling preserved.

We have also added the old style round oven which was always a necessary adjunct to these old Cotswold homes.

During our dismantling operations we shall endeavour to tone down such new parts as we have been compelled to add, until they are in keeping with the original portions of the building.

The days in England are rapidly shortening, and we should very much like to complete the shipment of this building before the real Winter sets in, and with this thought in mind, perhaps you will very kindly cable us any instructions you may have concerning its dismantling or further modification.

Yours truly,

F. Morton.

HM HL

PLEASE ADDRESS ALL COMMUNICATIONS
TO THE COMPANY AND NOT TO INDIVIDUALS

along to help with reconstruction in the village during the summer of 1930. Although Cutler felt the "experts" proved more trouble than they were worth, the cottage and barn, complete with Cotswold sheep and doves, stood south of Secretary House by the end of September (13). The changes described in Morton's letter to Frank Campsall (14) are apparent when compared to the pre-restoration photograph (11).

Since he had procured Cotswold sheep, Ford felt the picture incomplete without a sheepdog. Ernest Liebold located an authentic strain in Sault Sainte Marie, Ontario. For $75 he bought "Rover" (15), who became "the most faithful dog that we had ever seen," Liebold remembered. "He protected the few sheep around there and he was the master of that whole place."

14

15

13

SIR JOHN BENNETT

BENNETTS
RE BUILDING
SALE

65 SIR JOHN BENNETT Ld 65

WORLD-FAMED
WATCHES,
Sir JOHN BENNETT Ltd
CLOCKS
JEWELLERY

The Cotswold Forge, built c. 1600 and operated continuously for more than 300 years, arrived a year after the cottage. Ford and Morton found it in the village of Snowshill, Worcestershire, in the fall of 1930.

Another English building that caught Ford's fancy was the Sir John Bennett Jewelry Store from London. When Bennett moved into the building in 1846, he had replicas of the mythical giants Gog and Magog installed in the third-floor clock mechanism (16). The movable giants came down, amid considerable press coverage, for shipment to Dearborn with the rest of building during the winter of 1930-31 (17). Cutler scaled down the five-story building to fit the rest of the village setting (18), bowing to the old New England custom that no structure could be higher than the church steeple. Gog and Magog continue to strike the quarter hour in their new home.

Craft and small industrial buildings settled into the village in 1932. The 1810 Hanks Silk Mill from Mansfield, Connecticut, significant because it produced the first machine-made silk in America, featured machinery rebuilt from original drawings. The 1785 Kingston, New Hampshire, Cooper Shop became the oldest American craft shop in the village.

Sawmills were not only important to the village setting, they were used extensively by Cutler's crew to provide lumber for numerous construction and re-erecting projects. The 1855 Tripp Sawmill from Lenawee County, Michigan, featured an up-and-down saw (19) similar to one Henry Ford had operated in his youth. The original machinery produced lumber cut 19th-century style – invaluable for accurate restorations.

Prior to the dedication and for several years afterward, a circular sawmill operated near the museum (20, right). A two-story, frame chemical research laboratory rose next to it about 1930. Ford and his associates tested countless ways to use soybeans here, periodically adding to the building until the experiments moved to other Ford facilities in 1941. The lab stayed behind to house village service operations.

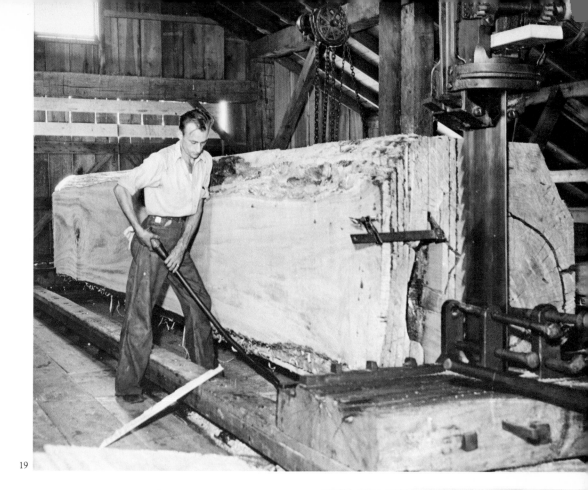

19

20

One of the first additions bearing strong Ford personal association was the 1933 replica of the Detroit workshop where he built his first car (21, original site; 22 and 23, village reconstruction). To get his Quadricycle out of the shed at 58 Bagley Avenue in 1896, Ford had to knock out the bricks around the doorway. After some bricklayer friends patched up Henry's "remodeling," the two doors of the structure differed in size. Although the original shed was torn down in later years, Ford located the house in which the bricks had been used. By building a new wall for the owners of the house, Ford was allowed to remove the old shed bricks for his reconstruction.

21

23

22

24

25

26

Diverse early modes of transportation abounded in Greenfield Village, including numerous horse-drawn vehicles. In addition to the Rocket and the President locomotives on the railroad siding, Edison's electric train ran across from the Menlo Park Laboratory for a few years, with Francis Jehl as engineer (24, Jehl with jacket).

Man, however, did not travel by road and rail alone in America's early years. Ford sought to fill an important transportation gap—water travel—by rebuilding the Suwanee, a 19th-century river steamer that Thomas Edison had frequently ridden in Florida. The boat sank there, however, and all Ford could salvage was the engine. During the summer of 1929, he brought the boat's one-time captain, Conrad Menge, to Dearborn to rebuild the boat. During Henry Ford's lifetime, the Suwanee saw little service (25), firing up only for special occasions. By the time of the dedication of the Stephen Foster Memorial in 1935, the third deck and pilot house had been removed and the second deck redesigned. In March 1937 Ford dredged a loop of the Rouge River abandoned when the stream changed course to create a circular Suwanee Lagoon (26). Still, the stern-wheeler sat idle much of the time. Its day was coming, however.

87

A Tribute to Edison

Thomas Edison died on October 18, 1931, almost two years to the day after he was honored by Ford and the world at Light's Golden Jubilee. Henry Ford's 1931 eulogy of his friend and hero paints a poignant picture.

Mr. Edison was a truly great man. He changed the face of the world in his lifetime, and everything he achieved was beneficial to mankind. The epoch created by his work will influence all the future. His fame is independent of the fluctuating judgments of history; it is etched in light and sound on the daily and hourly life of the world.

I knew him for nearly 40 years. He was the chief hero of my boyhood and he became my friend in manhood. That experience must be rare — to have one's early hero for one's later friend. The first encouraging word I ever had from any informed person on the making of a gasoline automobile was given me by Mr. Edison.

Great as an inventor, he was greater as a man. He knew the secret of work. His persistence amounted to genius. However much he originally owed to inspiration for his ideas, he developed them through tireless experiment and downright hard work.

His guiding principle was to make life better for human beings. His honesty was rugged, he had great courage and a lively sense of humor, but so rounded was his character that no trait stood out above the rest.

Mr. Edison was a deeply religious man in the highest sense of that word. He knew so much of the marvel and mystery of the universe that he reverenced it and the purpose behind it. He did some work for which the world is not yet ready. In foresight and insight he was a prophet.

Latterly he turned his mind to economic questions because he believed the present system hindered the best in men. He thoroughly believed that an economic improvement which must come is a closer relation between agriculture and industry. He was convinced that our money machinery was badly in need of attention.

Mr. Edison believed that the essential individual life survived the change called death. We often spoke of it together. Faith with him was a real evidence of things not seen. Mr. Edison himself did not grow old. He was like a young driver in a worn-out car. He has just gone, I believe, to get new facilities to continue his work. But the sense of personal loss is very heavy. There was only one Edison.

Opening the Gates

Between 1929 and 1933, activity flourished in both the village and museum. Buildings for the village seemed to be pouring in, artifacts were transferred from Building 13 to the museum and preliminary cataloging and arrangement of exhibits began. The village school system was growing as fast as its children. The public, notified by the October 21 broadcast and numerous articles in the nation's periodicals, knew well that Henry Ford had something amazing going on behind his handmade brick walls. The few curious passersby a day grew to about 400 a day early in the 1930s. Those given permission for a village tour set out in groups of 25 with student guides about every 15 minutes. No one was admitted to the unfinished museum without a special pass. By the late spring of 1933, however, a curious public had swelled to nearly 1,000 pairs of inquiring eyes each day. To turn this many people away simply amounted to bad public relations. Incorporating suggestions from William Simonds, Ford secretary Frank Campsall made the following recommendations to his boss:

To operate Greenfield Village in a manner that will permit the visitor to feel as if he or she had been transported back a few years and was seeing a community for the first time, it should be so arranged that they are not herded through in groups with a guide having a set "lingo" which becomes monotonous and detracts from the true atmosphere of the historic town.

Visitors should be charged admission, adults 25 cents, children 10 cents. Children under 16 in groups accompanied by teachers or supervisors could be admitted without charge under the guest privilege of a visiting student.

The buildings of the Village now partially completed should be finished and opened to view. The Steinmetz Study, Burbank's Office and the Secretary Pearson House could all be put in order in a short time.

The Kingston Cooper Shop could be used as Herb Forbes' Wheelwright Shop or for restoration on wood items, he could have one or two students help.

The Currier Shoe Shop could be occupied by a student of the shoemaker.

Mr. Tremear with Jack Jackson could return to the Tintype Studio.

The Post Office should be occupied by [a] mail clerk to handle mailing and postage, the sale of Greenfield Village flour and products of the Carding Mill, besides the sale of cards and special booklets, or this could be handled separately at the Waterford Country Store, which should be occupied by an old time storekeeper.

At the Clinton Inn should be a typical old time hotel keeper and like all early towns should be the receiving center. The visitors, entering carriages at the "Waiting Room" after purchasing ticket[s], would drive to the Inn and then check surplus clothing or articles and be made acquainted with the character of the Village by the Innkeeper, who arranges for guides with each group (similar to Wayside Inn Bar Room activity).

Mr. Simonds has suggested a relay system of guiding which I believe is quite practical for present requirements. That is, the Village is "zoned." One guide proceeds with his group, for instance, around the "Common" and at the Town Hall turns them over to another guide who covers the "Menlo Park Buildings," he in turn at the Jordan House leaves them with a third guide who conducts the group through the buildings in that locality. At the Cotswold the carriages can pick up passengers and bring to a fourth guide at the Post Office who continues the group toward the exit. This type of program would be quite different from the usual routine handling of guests and until such time as the Village is complete when the visitors could go without guides as they now do in visiting an ordinary town.

Refreshments — buffet luncheons — should be served at the Clinton Inn by the students of hotel and restaurant work. A hostess should be located at the Waiting Room and a nurse selected for the month or season located at the Clinton Inn who could also serve as hostess there.

The Blacksmith Shop should have an extra man, one capable of making colonial iron work. (Mr. Arndt has such a man named Peterson.)

The guides should be carefully selected Trade School boys 17-18 years of age who are assigned for only the season. Should any of them be found who will fit in the Village industries, they can be so absorbed into the activities and the rest continue on at the Trade School.

The Glass Blower should be producing small articles for sale in the Country Store or Post Office.

27

Evidently plans to admit visitors were in mind at least a year before the gates opened. In the summer of 1932, construction began on the village "gates," the colonial-style waiting room. That fall two public restrooms went up just inside the perimeter wall. By mid-May 1933 the gatehouse (as it was later called) awaited the first eager feet to pass through into the streets of America's past (27).

Ford approved the basic substance of Frank Campsall's and William Simonds' suggestions for opening the village to the public. On June 22, 1933, the first "public" visitors began climbing in and out of the horse-drawn omnibuses for a look at Ford's outdoor history book of the common man (28, June 1933).

As Campsall's memorandum pointed out, crafts played an important role in village operations, even before the public was admitted. Glassblowers produced some of the village's first souvenir items (29). The Tintype Studio became a popular stop for visitors. For a nominal sum, tintypist Charles Tremear (30) provided an antique-appearing likeness of visitors, dressed in costumes of their choosing. Famous guests (31, Walt Disney) usually could not resist.

28

29

30

31

32

Activity around the Loranger Grist Mill gave the public a colorful picture of an earlier age (32). Inside, the two large stone grinding wheels could turn out one barrel of flour (whole wheat or buckwheat) or corn meal an hour. Some of the milled grain was used locally, some went into the village school-children's lunches, and the rest was packaged in three-pound sacks and sold to the public.

Another segment of the public gained admittance only by invitation – to wedding ceremonies in the village chapel. Martha-Mary Chapel hosted the first of thousands of weddings on June 22, 1935.

By 1936 the gatehouse had to be enlarged. The crowds exceeded expectations, causing discontinuation of such routine services as transfer of visitors to the Clinton Inn via horse-drawn carriages. The new wing housed a guide study room, locker facilities, a storage area and glass cases displaying village craft items. In addition, the enlarged structure provided room for a special guest reception area and William Simonds' office. A private gate cut into the fence admitted important village visitors.

91

A Pictorial Map of

EDISON INSTITUTE MUSEUM & HISTORICAL GREENFIELD VILLAGE

LOCATED AT DEARBORN, MICHIGAN

★

FOUNDED BY HENRY FORD

★

OPEN TO THE PUBLIC

★

Those entering the village found considerable ground to cover, as early maps indicated (33, 1934). Efforts to feed the throngs had begun shortly after the dedication when the 1890s "Owl" Night Lunch Wagon from Detroit opened (34). Henry Ford used to frequent the stand when he worked the night shift at the Edison Illuminating Company.

The Owl's task was eased when the Dearborn Inn was built in 1931, a few hundred yards southwest of the institute on Oakwood Boulevard (35). Designed by Detroit architect Albert Kahn, the inn was one of the world's first airport hotels, serving airline passengers landing at Ford Airport across the street. For additional lodgings, Ford in 1937 reproduced the homes of five famous Americans – Walt Whitman, Edgar Allan Poe, Barbara Fritchie, Patrick Henry and Oliver Wolcott – behind the inn.

35

36

The museum was in various stages of completion when the first visitor walked through its doors in 1933, about a week after the village opened. The entrance hall would look much the same for a number of years (36, 1936).

The decorative arts displays had progressed further than the mechanical arts exhibits in the back (37), but were often still temporary (38). The first plan for the decorative arts galleries entailed placing the earliest artifacts in corridor A and moving chronologically across the corridors, with 20th-century objects occupying corridor E (39). By 1935, a number of pieces stood in the corridors, but placements would later change.

For the great expanse of the rear exhibition hall, Cutler and museum "boss" Fred Smith submitted plans for placement of cases and artifact groupings to Ford (40, circles on the grid represent ceiling support columns).

For some objects, there was no question about location. When the President was run in on the rails in December 1933, it appeared to be the only object in that area of the museum (41). Laying of the teak floor, a painstaking process, would not be completed in all areas until 1938. A "street" of early American shops began to take shape in 1931, the first such installation in an American museum. Ed Cutler designed the Celotex mock-ups (42).

38

37

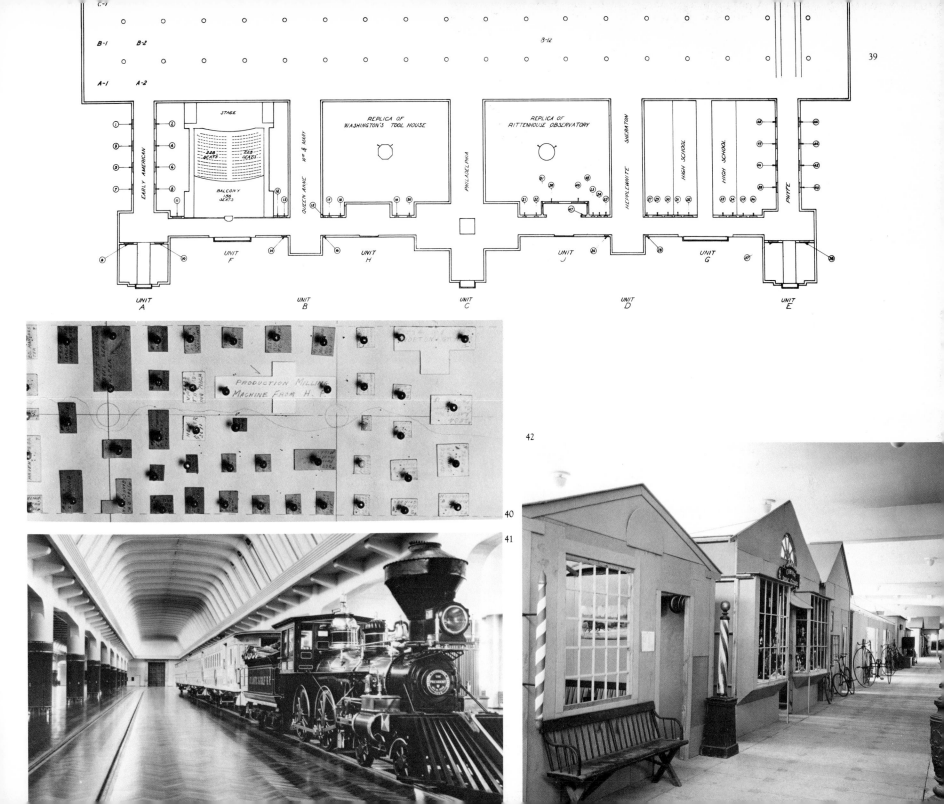

Certain personalities surfacing in the early 1930s would wield considerable influence over village and museum operations. Henry Ford always remained in charge, but he could not be everywhere. Even as early as 1930, much of the staff for the next decade or so began to come together (43, at the Clinton Inn, left to right: William J. Cameron, Ford personal spokesman and public relations man; Ray Dahlinger, head of the Ford Farms; Jim Sweinhart, N. W. Ayers Advertising Company representative; Frank Campsall; M. Sipple, former caretaker of Ford Homestead and personal village purchasing and personnel aide to Ford; Evangeline Dahlinger, wife of Ray Dahlinger, active in village schools operations; Conrad Menge, former captain of the *Suwanee* and her building consultant; George Burns, Henry Ford's driver; Fred Miller, museum custodian; Herb Forbes, wheelwright who also assisted Menge; and Fred Smith, museum custodian).

In 1934, responsibilities, if not lines of authority, were laid out in black and white (44). The most powerful men working specifically for the institute seemed to be Ed Cutler, Ray Dahlinger (45), Fred Smith (46), Fred Miller (47) and William Simonds (48).

Since many of the village workmen came from the ranks of Ford farm laborers, Ray Dahlinger maintained an ever-growing control over village operations. Fred Smith gradually took charge of the museum after Jimmy Humberstone left. Originally Smith's boss, Fred Miller reportedly was hard of hearing and Smith began answering the phone for him. Smith's relaying of orders from Henry Ford soon established his power. Simonds ran many of the day-to-day visitor operations in the village and supervised the guides in the museum until he came up against Smith. As Simonds remembered:

> We had a man who was in charge, an older guide, and under him a staff, and it worked out very well until it got to the point when Fred Smith insisted that it would be necessary for him to take over the direction of the guides because they were getting into things and making trouble for him, and not handling people properly, and various other reasons. So there was no advantage in quarreling about it. We were very happy to have him take care of it. After that, for some reason, the museum seemed to run very smoothly. The same boys that were bothering him worked out very well.

43

THE EDISON INSTITUTE

President	Vice President	Secretary & Treasurer	Assistant Secretary & Treasurer
Henry Ford	Clara B Ford	Edsel B Ford	E G Liebold

Supervision Personnel & Purchases
Frank Campsall

Accounting & Finance
L J Thompson

Supervision Construction & Grounds --- Ray Dahlinger
Manager of Guides - Public Relations --- Wm A Simonds
Follow-up --- M H Sipple
Superintendent of Museum Building - Fred Smith) 20 Men - janitors & service
Receiving & Shipping - Service - Fred Miller)
Collectors - W W Taylor --- Charles T Newton --- J W Bishop (Electrical)
Engineering Maintenance --- Charles Voorhess --- Russell Mills --- Hans Press
    Electrician --- Ernest Eyres
    Power House --- Charles Fereau --- R Dunn --- M Walker --- Relief Williams
    Carpenter --- Ernest Foster --- Jess
Rigging & Erection of Mechanical Exhibits --- Roy Schuman
Building & Construction --- Wm Kanack
Planning & Layout --- Ed Cutler

School & Music --- B B Lovett
Old-time Orchestra & Dance Instruction)

Scotch Settlement	--- Miss Webster
Town Hall	--- Miss Mason
Clinton Inn	--- Mrs Cadaret
High Schools	--- Mr Grophear
	--- Miss Trebilcock
Secretary's House	--- Miss Mackinnon
Voice	--- Mr Koch
Riding School	--- Capt Armstrong

Instructor in Woodwork --- Wm Fry
Instructor in Mechanics --- Jack Dewar

Curator of Menlo Park	---	Francis Jehl
Edison Machine Shop	---	Henry Knope
Saw Mill	---	C Penrod
Glass Plant	---	J Olsen
Chemical Plant	---	R A Boyer
Tin Type Studio	---	Charles Tremear
Horse Barn & Teamsters	---	Oscar Smith
Chapel Organist	---	Earl A Tank
Flour Mill	---	R K Shackleton
Armington & Sims (Engine Repair)	---	Wm Miller
Lapeer Shop - Cabinet Work	---	Frank Toth
Wheelwright	---	Herb Forbes
Sir John Bennett Shop	---	Mr Castell
Watches - Engineering Lab	---	R Love
Woodwork & Boats	---	Capt Menge
Whittier Toll House - Shoemaker	---	
Blacksmith	---	Mr Anderson
Cooper Shop	---	
Village Service	---	Wm Theisen - Gate Me Watchmen

44

45   46   47   48

The Village as Classroom

Since September 1929, with or without visitors or construction work, children in the Greenfield Village schools were learning the three Rs—and then some. Henry Ford envisioned the entire complex as an educational institution, with students using the artifacts and exhibits for practical learning experiences. Some parts of the dream came true more successfully than others in the last 18 years of his life.

As the original students in the Scotch Settlement School grew older, Ford added grades and buildings to accommodate them. The following list gives the opening year and location of the various levels in the system:

KINDERGARTEN
Ann Arbor House, 1937
Edison Homestead, 1944

PRIMARY GRADES
Scotch Settlement School, 1929
Town Hall, 1930
Clinton Inn, 1933 (one year only)
McGuffey School, 1934
Secretary House, 1941
Miller School, 1943

SECONDARY GRADES
Edison Institute High School (Museum), 1934

COLLEGE LEVEL
Edison Institute of Technology (Recreation Building), 1937

By 1930, The Edison Institute faculty had doubled—from one to two. For the fall 1932 term, two new teachers replaced the previous two. One new arrival was E. Lucile Webster, who continued teaching until the village schools closed in 1969. Webster, spending most of those years in the one-room Scotch Settlement School, recalled her hiring in her autobiography:

> I spent a very interesting day in Greenfield Village and had dinner with Mr. Lovett in Mr. Henry Ford's private dining room, then located in the Ford Engineering Laboratory . . . . After dinner and before I left that day, Mr. Lovett hired me to teach in the village in the fall with the understanding that I must keep my long hair and not cut it later. There

was not a contract, but simply a verbal agreement. I was to work seven days a week, if needed, and was to be on duty 24 hours if necessary. It was a challenge for me to work in the spacious outdoor museum of Americana for the sum of $200 per month with a two-week vacation sometime during the summer months.

Teaching in a restored 19th-century building had its drawbacks, although Henry Ford made periodic improvements, as Webster remembered:

> On a dark day the six antique kerosene wall lamps were not adequate light for the children. Whenever there was a storm or a dark winter day, I taught by the lecture method, because the light was poor. This was soon corrected by indirect lighting which was reflected from electric ceiling lights.

Experiences for the children were remarkable in their variety. Carroll Jean Lewis, a student in the system during the late 1930s and 1940s, spent an evening with Henry and Clara Ford during a week's live-in home economics class at Webster House.

> We were sitting in the front parlor and Mr. Ford was discussing the new bomber plant at Willow Run. Apparently we girls were not responding well to his new venture and he suddenly realized that we probably didn't know anything at all about bombers or how they were assembled. Immediately this was rectified, for from then on, each Thursday morning the group of Webster House girls was taken by service car out to the bomber plant and given a first-hand tour . . . . How the boys would have enjoyed such a trip, but they were never given the opportunity. Perhaps Mr. Ford felt the boys already knew all about such assembly line practices, or perhaps he didn't want his boys to have to know about bombers at that time, during World War II.

Learning by doing was Ford's overriding educational philosophy. Thus, a child's village schooling included informal field trips, paid work-study programs and classes in a one-room school, in which older children helped younger ones. William Simonds, in his 1938 book, *Henry Ford and Greenfield Village*, expressed the depth of possible experience:

"Learning by Doing" might be glimpsed in a project carried out by older boys and girls studying pioneer development. A 75-year-old log cabin in Greenfield Village became their laboratory. One committee drew floor plans. Another laid out the rooms on the floor of the museum and from the vast collection of Americana, selected furnishings that seemed appropri-

ate to such a log cabin in the Midwest a century ago. Each article was considered carefully, and discarded if not in keeping with the times and circumstances. After the instructor had finally approved their choice, the furnishings were set up in the cabin itself. Then the pupils met one evening at the cabin and ate a dinner cooked on the old wood stove by the girls of the class.

No tuition was charged. Henry Ford paid for everything. Chosen students came from a waiting list representing a variety of backgrounds and were not necessarily related to Ford Motor Company employees. Although a committee decided who would attend, Ford often added children after personal requests. He provided supplies, transportation (usually bus, although sometimes private cars or, occasionally in the winter, horse-drawn sleighs) and lunches served on linen tablecloths with matching napkins.

Enrollment climbed from 32 in 1929, to 190 in 1937, when the first high school class graduated, and to 300 in 1940. Yet even before Ford's death in April 1947, the program's scope diminished. Most of the outlying schools that Ford operated had been sold. The Edison Institute of Technology, the three-year, work-study engineering college, closed in 1943 because of the war. In 1946, only 11th and 12th graders participated in the high school work-study program. After 1947, the schools sorely missed Ford's personal interest and support. By 1952, the high school closed, ending a fascinating era during which hundreds of fortunate children had learned Ford's byword: "learning is living and living cannot be learned from books alone."

51   52   53

50

49

(49) Benjamin B. Lovett, Ford's old-fashioned dancing master and director of the school system from its inception in 1929 through the early 1930s

(50) Carl Hood, supervisor of schools (including all country schools), 1936-45

(51) Mark Stroebel, teacher (1936-52), schools' principal (1952-69) and manager of School Services Department (1969-75)

(52) Miss E. Lucile Webster, primary grades teacher, 1932-69

(53) Margaret Papp McAlister, hired personally by Henry Ford while still in high school to teach in the Green Lane Academy pre-school (Macon / Tecumseh, Michigan) in 1933, transferring to the village schools in 1943, teaching weaving, arts and crafts through 1969, finally joining the Education Department after the schools closed

54

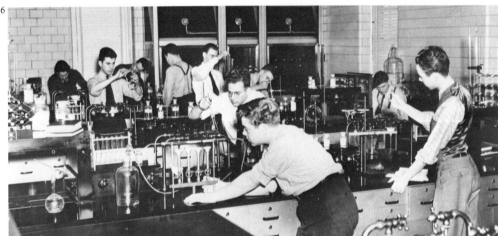

56

Village buses picked up students bright and early (54, April 1937). Opening day for Scotch Settlement School pupils came on September 16, 1929, more than a month before the village and museum dedication.

High school classrooms were located on either side of corridor G (see museum layout, page 95). Upstairs (55), rooms were designated with the letters E, D, I, S, O or N. Professional staff offices replaced the classrooms after the high school closed. Downstairs, the high school science lab became the Garden Room Restaurant and, later, the museum Book and Souvenir Shop.

Adjacent to the museum, in the new Recreation Building, 36 technical students (29 men and 7 women) got down to work on September 18, 1937. Each student earned money, alternating practical work experience with classroom and laboratory study (56) in mechanical, electrical, chemical and agricultural engineering.

Ann Arbor House kindergarten students had a lot to tell Mom and Dad after their first day, September 8, 1937 (57). Kindergarteners stayed all day at the village schools and helped to prepare their own lunches.

55

57

58

59

Beginning in 1930, each day opened with a brief, non-denominational service in Martha-Mary Chapel. Ford often watched from the balcony, frequently accompanied by famous guests, such as Will Rogers and George Washington Carver.

For a number of years, a national radio network put the services on the air one day a week. The village student chorus also performed on the Ford Sunday Evening Hour program, broadcast either from the chapel or from Detroit's Masonic Temple Auditorium.

Musical instruction was not limited to the voice. Benjamin Lovett's ballroom and old-fashioned dancing classes, taught in the Engineering Lab, were required subjects for village schoolchildren. After the erection of Lovett Hall in 1937, dances were held in the upstairs ballroom. Eventually, other Dearborn and then Detroit schoolchildren received instruction from more experienced village students.

Each student worked a vegetable garden plot in the village, taking home the fruits of his or her labor (58). Sales of surplus produce at a roadside stand, located at the intersection of Village and Southfield roads, netted profits for the students. During the Depression, the harvests proved especially welcome as did earnings, which one year amounted to $25 for each of 163 students.

Other school-related activities showed that learning could be fun. The Secretary House home economics instruction, for example, could provide delicious diversions (59, making the final table preparations for a Thanksgiving party in 1934). Boys found amusement in the experimental radio station behind the museum which the institute operated for several years. And what would spring be without baseball (60, 1935)? Both sexes enjoyed a Christmas season trip to Santa's Workshop at Ford's Fair Lane estate, while skating and sledding in the village occupied winter recesses.

Clara Ford wanted the children to be taught horseback riding. Classes met after school in the spring and fall and during summer vacations.

The children's annual May Festival, later resurrected as Country Fair of Yesteryear, marked the village's first special event. Amid the pageantry of Highland dances and mock equestrian maneuvers, Carol Bryant was crowned the first May Festival Queen in 1930 (61).

Despite his busy schedule, the proximity of his activities in the Engineering Lab, the Rouge plant and his home, Fair Lane (62, top, center, 1936), made village visits fairly easy for Ford (63).

62

60

61

101

63

64

While work on the teak floor progressed, the artifacts gradually jelled as exhibits. Looking toward the back of the hall, agricultural displays (64) occupied the far left. Object categories to the right included craft and home arts, industrial machinery, steam and electric power, communications, lighting and, finally, transportation farthest to the right. Arranging the mass of items was no easy task since Ford had few specific exhibition ideas in mind when he was collecting. The evolved pattern entailed arranging all objects of a certain type chronologically, thus permitting the visitor to observe minute changes in technology and design over the years. Explanatory labels looked haphazard at best (65, on stanchions). The Street of Early American Shops, illustrating trades, crafts and businesses of the 18th and 19th centuries, remained incomplete in 1937.

Up front, in the decorative arts galleries, exhibits seemed essentially in place by the early 1940s. The furniture and other home furnishings lining the corridors, wall cases and alcoves (66) demonstrated the successive styles and tastes of American craftsmen and manufacturers.

66

65

68   Collecting did not stop when the museum doors opened. *Significant objects acquired before Ford's death include: a c. 1709 Antonio Stradivari violin (67); a guitar used by Stephen Foster (68); the Victorian rocking chair in which Abraham Lincoln was shot while attending Ford's Theater in Washington, D.C. (69); the 1927 Junkers Bremen monoplane, the first plane to successfully fly the Atlantic east to west (70); a 1617-18 set of James I Apostle spoons made by an unknown London silversmith (71); a 1919 Excelsior motorcycle owned by Charles A. Lindbergh (72); and the Vought-Sikorsky-300 helicopter, the first such craft (on September 14, 1939) to make a successful flight (73, Igor Sikorsky lands his craft on the front lawn of the museum in 1943).*

67   69   71   72

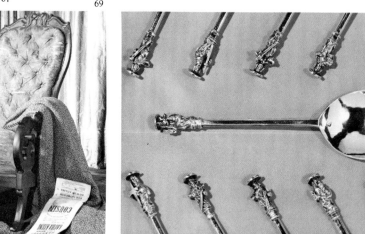

70   73

74

76

104

Scarcely a year passed between 1933 and 1947 without the
addition of two or three buildings to the bustling village. The
transfer of the Stephen Foster Memorial from Pittsburgh in
1934 prompted Pittsburgh Post-Gazette cartoonist Cyrus
Cotton Hungerford to ink the ''Pied Piper'' (74). Ford truly
was providing safe homes for the country's historic houses, as
many, the Foster building included, had fallen into terrible
condition or stood in dilapidated areas when he purchased them
(75, Ford and Frank Campsall on the porch steps).
Probably, most could not have survived for another decade on
their original sites. Once the historic houses were rescued in the
village, Ford restored them to their former splendor and
included such touches as a new generation of Foster's ''Old
Dog Tray'' (76, positioned on the banks of the Suwanee
Lagoon).

Part of Ford's original inclination toward the past stemmed
from a fondness for William Holmes McGuffey's Readers.
Collecting hundreds of copies was not enough. In 1934, he had
McGuffey's c. 1780 birthplace from Washington County,
Pennsylvania, re-erected on South Dearborn Road. That same
year, workers unloaded the original logs from an 18th-century
barn on the Holmes property at the village (77, village radio
towers and shack at rear) and used them to build a one-room
''McGuffey School'' (78). In September, McGuffey relatives
and other dignitaries gathered at the village to dedicate the
buildings.

Ford continued to realize his ideal of an educational
community by commissioning museum architect Robert O.
Derrick to construct a ''recreation building'' in 1936. When it
opened the following year, the structure housed the new Edison
Institute of Technology as well as a gymnasium and swimming
pool.

Village activity included more than just construction or
reconstruction, however. As in the case of the Clark House,
structures sometimes disappeared. Directly behind the
recreation building site, cleared in June 1936 (79), stood two
long horse barns, stabling nearly 100 animals. Ford farms
foreman Ray Dahlinger had charge of them. When Ford
discovered that village operations only employed about 25
horses, he ordered the barns removed. Within 24 hours, no
trace of the buildings remained and the ground was smoothly
graded.

77

78

79

82

81

83

80

84

Meanwhile, the new building, constructed mostly with imported materials, was taking shape. By July, the work crew had roughed in the pool (80). The scope of the job became apparent when the framing rose in September (81). The building boasted a completely original design, although it resembled the colonial architectural style of the adjacent museum. Through March and April, interior work included waterproofing the pool and building squash courts that Edsel Ford intended Ford Motor Company employees to use.

When the building officially opened on October 26, 1937, the major new addition to the institute sparkled (82). Following inspection of the building, a dedication dance commenced in the ballroom. Edsel Ford announced the ballroom would be called "Lovett Hall," in honor of Benjamin Lovett, Ford's old-fashioned dancing master since 1924, and his wife. Invited relatives, friends, motor company employees, village school-teachers and sometimes students attended the Lovett Hall dances, held nearly every two weeks (83).

Edison Institute high school students used the gym and pool (84), considered outstanding facilities for a school of its size. Other rooms included the technological institute's laboratories, a drafting room, a library, a machine shop and a spacious entrance lobby. After the institute of technology closed in 1943, the high school utilized more of the facilities until it, too, closed in 1952. The building, later called the Education Building and, finally, simply Lovett Hall, has since housed visiting school groups, adult education classes and institute offices.

Moving America's Buildings

Throughout his oral reminiscences, Edward Cutler (85) sprinkled tidbits concerning his procedures for dismantling and moving various historic structures:

There was no formal organization or administration of the village. My office was the head of the village. I used the men as I saw fit. In the formative years, to tear down a building, we used the village men. The furthest away we took the village men was to Lincoln [Postville], Illinois . . . when we took down the Lincoln Courthouse.

Ordinarily we picked up a bunch of laborers. In most cases, it depended where the building was located. When you get away down in Massachusetts, and you take the windmill, for instance, why, we used men from Cambridge, from the [Ford] branch [office]. You can get mechanics. When we worked it that way, why, we would get tools to handle things. The only place we couldn't get out branch men was the Webster House . . . we just had to hire local men there. I had to manage for that gang.

The first thing we do to preserve a building that we are going to tear down and move is to measure everything up thoroughly. Before you start to tear down anything, you make a lot of sketches to show the different details and the way things are arranged. You've got to do a thorough measurement job so there are no slip-ups, because you can't tear that down, put it all in a freight car, bring it in, and dump it off. You have to know what you are doing.

As you tear it down, you ordinarily numbered the pieces and marked where it had been, all the main pieces of construction; all the door frames, window frames, timbers, trusses, everything that meant construction, it was all numbered. Of course, you couldn't number siding or stuff like that, or bricks.

I'd always follow a job like that right down to the bottom. We'd tear the whole thing right down to the ground and bring it in piecemeal. Then, of course, the job begins to reconstruct it in the village.

The position to put the building was the thing that was always considered from every angle. I might suggest, but I never made any decisions. He [Ford] made the decisions, which was natural. It was his job, not mine. It was his property and his idea.

86

The dismantling and restoration of the 1822-23 New Haven, Connecticut, house in which Noah Webster wrote his dictionary, provided a good example of Ed Cutler's technique. Yale University planned to demolish the house, except for the louvered, elliptical window (which was to go to the Yale Art School) and the porch columns (which a descendant of the builder requested). One of Ford's dealers or agents brought the house's plight to his attention through Edsel (86). "The boss" purchased the Webster House from the university and told Cutler to bring it into the village.

When Cutler first reached New Haven in September 1936, wreckers had already demolished parts of the house. The second-story bay windows were additions removed by Cutler. The house's function as a college dormitory in later years may account for the interior's poor state of repair. Cutler jotted down notes and construction details of various sorts (87), then took pictures for future reference.

Once the men began dismantling, the house was down and packed up in two weeks, according to Cutler's estimate. "Now you get a gang of men on it, and you know what you want them to do, and you get them busy," Cutler said. "Of course you have got to do these things right, you can't go at them blunderingly." Whenever possible, the crew removed building materials in large pieces, making reassembly easier. Cutler worked fast; with his many projects, he had to.

In the village, the house went up during the winter of 1936-37 and soon looked much the way it did in Webster's day (88).

Later, Cutler recorded a written statement concerning dates of disassembly and reconstruction (89) as he did with most of the other historic buildings moved to the village. Throughout the 1940s, high school girls used the Webster House as a live-in home economics laboratory. It finally opened to the public in 1962, 140 years after its construction.

88

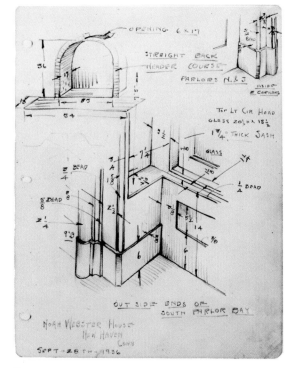

87

89

A New Stream for an Old Bridge

Seven miles from William McGuffey's birthplace, a covered bridge spanned Wheeling Creek between Pennsylvania's Washington and Greene counties. In the fall of 1937, it was a rotting, deteriorating vestige of the past (90). By the summer of 1938, it proudly connected the industrial and commercial sections of Greenfield Village with the residential, once again supporting modes of transportation that progress had left behind (91). The interesting story of the structure's road to the village is best related by the man in charge of the job, Roy Schumann:

90

91

When we arrived . . . they had had about eight inches of snow there which we had to go through.

We went outside, and it was about ten below zero. Up until that time it hadn't been very cold; the water wasn't frozen, and the roads weren't frozen. We went on the job that day and looked it over. The next morning we started out having trucks there.

We went ahead and started tearing down, marking things all up, taking off the rafters. First we tore the shingles off, tore the rafters off, and took the structure off. It stayed cold all the time we were there which was one of the best things for it because when we dropped a roof board on the river, the ice was there to catch it. All we had to do was pick it off.

It soon froze hard enough that we could get down there with our equipment. Fate evidently was with me because we had to shore up underneath the center of that bridge in order to take the timbers down.

We tore the whole thing down. I would say we were down there about three or four weeks. We got the timbers all out, everything cleaned off the ice that night. I told the men we wanted everything cleaned up. The next morning it rained, turned warmer, and took all the ice out of the river. If it had done that a day or two before or a week before, and that ice hadn't frozen to seven or eight inches thick, it would have taken the bridge and everything down the river, and I would have probably been down the river fishing timbers.

We had to dig all of the stones out of the bank and bring all the stones back with us here. We didn't number them. They were only rough four-inch stone, and wouldn't matter too much in what location they laid.

The timbers, of course, were numbered and went back to the place they originally came out. Then we had to haul this to Waynesburg, which was the closest railroad. That was about 25 miles. All of this had to be trucked in there, loaded on cars, and shipped up here.

The roads were icy, and you didn't know whether or not you would get to the top of the hill. We finally made it.

We went down there the first part of December and came back the 23rd of December. It was just two nights before Christmas when we got back.

Buildings multiplied on either side of the Ackley Covered Bridge. Cutler and about 50 boys from the Wayside Inn schools dismantled the c. 1800 Luther Burbank Birthplace in Lancaster, Massachusetts (92, frame portion at right), during the fall and winter of 1936. Cutler discovered that a later owner had split the frame building in half and constructed a brick house in the middle. Ford bought only the two original wings. Like most jobs, Cutler did this one in a hurry.

"In loading the brick out of the foundation, I had them [the boys] line up in a string and pass the brick. It was really funny. That brick came out of there faster than you could do it with a machine! They had a lot of fun playing, you know. I let 'em play. It was a game for them, and we were getting the work done." Ford's "learning by doing" philosophy could not have been illustrated better. By early summer 1937, horticulturalist Luther Burbank's house had a new home on South Dearborn Road (93).

In 1936, nationwide Ford dealers presented Henry Ford with a 17th-century Cape Cod windmill, thought to be the oldest standing windmill in the United States. Cutler and crew raised the stone foundation ten feet for safety precautions. Hundreds of dealers gathered on November 6, 1936, for the formal ceremony (94).

92

94

93

97

95

In the spring of 1942, workers completed a memorial to another man for whom Ford had tremendous respect and admiration – agricultural chemist George Washington Carver. The small log structure built near the village green end of South Dearborn Road was based on Carver's memories of his Diamond Grove, Missouri, plantation birthplace. Carver visited Henry and Edsel in July 1942 and spent a few days in the modest cabin.

The Carver Memorial completed a group of buildings that represented the progress of American blacks from bondage through emancipation to world recognition and leadership. In 1934, Ford had moved two small brick slave cabins from the Hermitage plantation near Savannah, Georgia (95), to a spot just behind the Lincoln Courthouse. The Carver building came next, followed in 1943 by the ante-bellum Mattox House, a plantation overseer's dwelling from Ways, Georgia.

112

96

98

The addition of the c. 1650 Susquehanna House from the bluffs of the Patuxent River in tidewater Maryland increased southern representation in the village. A relative of one of the original owner's descendants offered the house to Henry Ford in March 1942. When Cutler arrived to inspect it, the building was intact, but run down (96). Inside (97), he had to wade through 18 inches of grain to take his measurements. After viewing the drawings and photographs Cutler brought back, Ford decided to acquire this home of affluent colonial Maryland tax collector Christopher Rousby. Cutler moved the structure and erected it the same year. By August, complete with one of the country's oldest gravestones, the house was restored (98 and 99) and oriented to the compass as it had been in Maryland.

With all these major projects going on, Ford almost forgot an old friend—the 1860 Chapman House he had transferred to the village in 1929. On blocks for 11 years, the house finally found a permanent site in 1940, behind the Scotch Settlement School on South Dearborn Road (100).

99

100

Transplanting the Wright Brothers' 1870 birthplace and late 19th-century cycle shop from Dayton, Ohio, in 1937-38, probably ranks as the most significant village project of the 1930s. The Wrights had built their first plane in the bicycle sales and repair shop. Ford wanted it restored to its appearance of 1903, when the brothers took to the air at Kitty Hawk, North Carolina. Both Henry Ford and Orville Wright (Wilbur had died in 1912) were heavily involved in the project. Complete plans called for the display of the Wrights' first plane, but Ford could not swing the deal.

Ed Cutler, Orville Wright and Fred Black (101, right to left) and, of course, Henry Ford carefully surveyed the Victorian home (102, c. 1898).

The brick shop received similar attention from the two inventors. Wright and his one-time assistant Charles E. Taylor, who began working for the Wrights in 1901 and built the engine for their first plane, studied the drawings for accuracy (103, with Ford).

Reconstruction work progressed through 1937. The dedication ceremonies on April 16, 1938, more extravagant than usual, began with a reception at the Clinton Inn. The village school chorus performed at the formal outdoor ceremonies that followed for assembled guests and a radio audience. The day climaxed with a banquet for the dignitaries. The two buildings, meanwhile, had been meticulously restored inside and outside (104).

101

103

104

More commerical shops arrived in the late 1930s and early 1940s. The 1878 Grimm Jewelry Store, originally located on Michigan Avenue in Detroit, was placed on a site across the street from the Wright Cycle Shop in 1940 (105) adjacent to the Magill Jewelry Store where Henry Ford moonlighted as a young man, repairing watches. Ford and Englebert Grimm remained good friends until Grimm's death in 1931. Grimm wanted the contents of his store bequeathed to Henry Ford, and his surviving daughter complied with the request in 1932. Ford obtained the building itself from the city of Detroit (for a $195 salvage fee) several years later.

Ford augmented the village's industrial section with numerous agricultural mills, sawmills, machine shops and small factories such as the 1851 Richart Carriage Shop from Macon, Michigan, reconstructed in 1941 (106). Wagons and carriages reached the second floor, where craftsmen traditionally finished and painted them, via the outdoor ramp which Ford restored (107). Close by the carriage shop stood the village boiler-repair shop, a 1934 structure based on a 19th-century design.

Ford further enhanced the village's Edison collection with the 1941 addition of Building 11 from the inventor's 1886 West Orange, New Jersey, laboratory complex. At West Orange, ten times the size of his earlier Menlo Park facilities, Edison worked on improved recording and motion picture devices and other inventions. The restored building was placed just outside the Menlo Park Compound.

108

109

110

The last building Henry Ford moved to Greenfield Village was the first one he had preserved: his family homestead. Evidently its chances of survival in a developing area and the need for 24-hour security protection from vandals worried him. Because the proximity of the dwelling to the village did not warrant one of Cutler's magical disassemblies, it was simply cut in two and hauled over by truck (108). The village site awaited the main structure, with some of the outbuildings already in place (109). Available space did not permit transferral of all the barns and sheds. The completed homestead offered Ford quite a present the day before his 81st birthday (110, July 29, 1944). Cutler's first architectural job for "the boss," the Stover windmill, was removed several years after its reassembly in Greenfield Village.

Ford and Cutler joined forces in 1945 to construct one last building—a one-quarter-scale reproduction of Ford's first factory, the Ford Mack Avenue plant (111, original building; 112, 1944 construction of reproduction; and 113, a later move within the village). With the village virtually complete, Cutler left for the Rouge complex in 1946 and retired in 1947, the year of Henry Ford's death. Their two decades of fervent construction activity had given America a village of her past.

111

112

113

1—Parking Lot
2—The Edison Institute Museum
3—Gate Lodge Entrance
4—Floral Clock
5—Village Barn
6—Chemical Laboratory
7—Village Print Shop
8—Loranger Gristmill
9—Henry Ford Birthplace
10—Edsel Ford Building
11—Armington & Sims Machine Shop
12—Hanks Silk Mill
13—Deluge Fire House
14—Lunch Wagon
15—Plymouth Carding Mill
16—Weaving Shed
17—Blacksmith Shop
18—Kingston Cooper Shop
19—Currier Shoe Shop
20—Toll House
21—Tintype Studio
22—Post Office
23—Plymouth House
24—Riding Stable
25—Pioneer Log Cabin
26—Gardner House
27—Waterford General Store
28—Clinton Inn
29—Herb Garden
30—Martha-Mary Chapel
31—Steamer Suwanee
32—Scotch Settlement School
33—Logan County Courthouse
34—Slave Huts
35—George Washington Carver Memorial
36—Mattox House
37—Chapman House
38—George Matthew Adams Birthplace
39—Steinmetz Camp
40—McGuffey Group
41—Stephen Foster Birthplace

42—Swiss Watchmakers' Chalet
43—Luther Burbank Birth place
44—Ann Arbor House
45—Noah Webster House
46—Secretary House
47—Cotswold Group
48—Cotswold Forge
49—Cape Cod Windmill

50—Plympton House
51—Susquehanna House
52—Edison Homestead
53—Covered Bridge
54—Fort Myers Laboratory
55—Sarah Jordan Boarding House
56—Menlo Park Group
57—Building Number 11
58—Miller School

59—58 Bagley Avenue Shop
60—Magill Jewelry Store
61—Wright Cycle Shop
62—Wright Home
63—Grimm Jewelry Store
64—Sir John Bennett Jewelry Store
65—Town Hall
66—Smith's Creek Depot
67—Edison Illuminating Co.

68—Lapeer Machine Shop
69—Sandwich Glass Plant
70—Planing Mill
71—Sorghum Mill
72—Cotton Gin Mill
73—Rice Mill
74—Circular Sawmill
75—Spofford Sawmill
76—Cider Mill
77—Walking Beam Engine

78—Haycock Boiler
79—Boiler Shop
80—Mack Avenue Plant
81—Brick and Tile Works
82—Pottery Shop
83—Tripp Sawmill
84—Macon Carriage Shop
85—The Edison Institute High School
86—Luther Burbank Office
RR—Rest Rooms

AIR VIEW OF GREENFIELD VILLAGE, EDISON INSTITUTE

116   115

By 1947 Henry Ford had gathered nearly 90 historic and reproduction buildings depicting America's 17th, 18th, 19th and 20th centuries (114) and a massive museum building filled to the brim with the artifacts Americans made and used to carry them into the 20th century. Woven through these incredible resources were the village school system and Ford's founding purpose: education. What he had built, others would build upon.

The passing of one of The Edison Institute's three founders on May 26, 1943, dealt a serious blow to the future of the institute. Edsel Ford (115, July 1942) gave considerable support to what he regarded as strictly his father's project, and Henry undoubtedly expected Edsel to take over after his own death. One of Edsel's greatest legacies, however, was his family, two of whose members would become chief executive officers of The Edison Institute (116, left to right: Edsel, his wife Eleanor Clay, Henry II, Benson, Josephine and William Clay).

Some of Edsel's donations to the institute included: a c. 1770 silver coffee pot made by Paul Revere (117), c. 1770 plaster busts of Franklin and Washington (118 and 119), and the Floyd Bennett Ford Tri-Motor (not pictured).

In the year after his only son's death, Henry Ford built a memorial to him in the village. Based on Edsel's second-floor garage workshop, located at the Ford's Edison Avenue home, the brick structure was dedicated on December 24, 1944 (120, inside the memorial, left to right: J. W. Thompson; B. J. Craig, a future Edison Institute trustee; Frank Campsall; C. E. Sorensen; Henry Ford; Ray Dahlinger; and Henry Ford II, Edsel's eldest son).

118 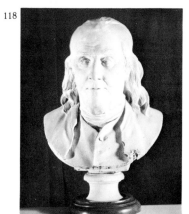 119

117  120

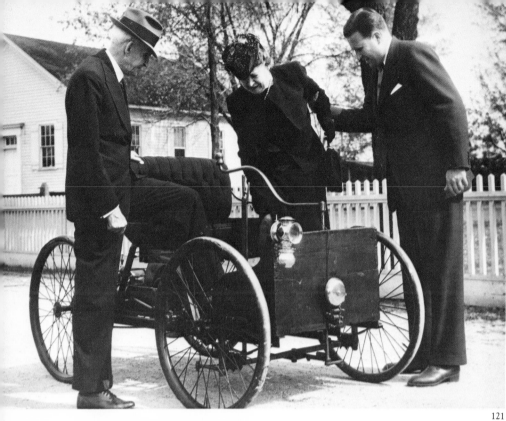

121

123

122

On May 26, 1946, *assisted by grandson Henry II and accompanied by his wife Clara, Ford took one last spin through the village in the Quadricycle, the vehicle that made The Edison Institute and all of Ford's enterprises possible (121). Less than a year later, on April 7, 1947, Henry Ford died in his Fair Lane home. While his body lay in state in Lovett Hall, more than 100,000 people filed past in tribute (122). He was buried on April 10 in the family plot on Joy Road near Greenfield Road in Detroit. In the years since, village school students and museum administrators annually have commemorated his death with a graveside service.*

Henry Ford (123, c. 1934), the complex man both scoffed at and honored for his contributions to the preservation of America's past, had created an educational institution of amazing depth and resources. Beyond a doubt, Ford left his unique mark on the institute he created, from involving his family in its development (124, with Edsel in the Plympton House, 1941), to overseeing construction, to interpreting the artifacts he had gathered, to educating children by encouraging his philosophy of learning by doing (125, in the village, 1937, from left to right: Ann Hood, the school superintendent's daughter; Roy Schumann; Ed Cutler; and Jean Schumann, Roy's daughter).

1948-1954

We do not make changes for the sake of making them, but we never fail to make a change once it is demonstrated that the new way is better than the old way.

— HENRY FORD

Chapter Five

Transition

I'll never forget the first day that I came in. They took me back to . . . the accounting offices . . . and introduced me. Then I started to walk around the museum and see who was here and who wasn't here. And, much to my surprise, I found Fred Smith ensconced way in the back of the museum . . . and he had one girl . . . . And then in the forward part of the museum there were the servicemen, guards. I can't remember the exact number, but they were much fewer in number than they should have been. But, outside of those two people in the back room, the only person I found working in the museum was Bill Distin. And that was the extent of any office force or professional help, or curatorial staff . . . that was it. So, for about three weeks I continually walked around and around the museum from one end to the other. Of course I came in in February and there were no people in the museum. If we had 25 a day, that was a crowd, until springtime came when the . . . school groups started to come. So my first question that propounded itself was, what am I going to do? Where do I begin? Where do I start?

Hayward S. Ablewhite, ''Reminiscences''

So stood the situation in February 1949 when The Edison Institute Board of Trustees appointed Hayward S. Ablewhite director of the museum. The new director found Henry Ford's incredible historical resources almost dormant. The village remained completely closed during the winter months except for the schools.

What had happened since Ford's death two years earlier? A consultant's report, commissioned in 1947, summarized the state of the village and museum after studying similar institutions across the country: "The Edison Institute museums (including the Museum Building and Greenfield Village) have probably the largest existing collection of authentic material illustrating the industrial and cultural development of the country, including manufacturing, agriculture, transportation, communication, and the applied arts." The report continued:

By the appropriate organization of this material and operation of the institute in accordance with a predetermined objective, these museums can make an educational contribution surpassing that of any other institutions in the museum field. Such a goal would be worthy of the founder of the institute and should merit the lasting gratitude of all American citizens.

The answer to the question of what had happened to the institute since Ford's death was: very little. The report's suggested objective did not differ from Henry Ford's own broad educational ideas, stated many times through the years. Basically, the staff was simply maintaining the status quo, fulfilling its duties with no direction other than trying to continue what it felt Mr. Ford would have wanted.

The operation of the complex had fallen to Clara Ford in 1947. As Ablewhite remembered, "No one else had anything to do with it . . . . But she would come over . . . at least once a week . . . and would be very disturbed if she thought you had any ideas of changing anything that she would think contrary to what Mr. Ford's ideas for the museum were."

A picture of Ford's unquestionably total control of the village and museum emerges in comments by two of his closest aides. "Henry Ford was not an organization man," according to Fred Black. Ernest G. Liebold explained:

> He looked after the detail work of erecting the buildings and so on. Of course, when Mr. Ford did that, it obviated the necessity of anyone else taking any general supervision over it, because Mr. Ford had his own ideas of how he wanted things done, and you were liable to get in difficulty if you tried to use your own judgment.

Ford's subordinates at the village and museum in those days possessed varying degrees of influence but never wielded official control or authority. Although some built small empires beneath them, they always had to depend on Ford's support when a dispute arose. Thus, remaining in Ford's good graces proved vital to their survival. An official chain of command never emerged. The two men with the greatest unofficial power during the 1940s were Ray Dahlinger in the village and Fred Smith in the museum. Their strong influence extended into the early 1950s, causing a number of conflicts within the new organizational structure then evolving.

1948-1954

Without ready access to the tremendous resources Henry Ford commanded, however, the staff could not hope to run the institute in the same fashion. Unimaginative holdovers from the Henry Ford years administered the village and museum separately, with different staffs, on a day-to-day basis. The payroll office provided the only common denominator between the two facilities. The inevitable disruptive change from Ford's solitary rule surfaced with Ablewhite's appointment and continued after Clara Ford's death in September 1950. Affairs had steadied by the beginning of Donald A. Shelley's term as executive director in November 1954.

Improvements began in 1950 with the drafting of the institute's first organizational chart. Emil A. Ulbrich, in the newly created position of Edison Institute general manager, answered to the board of directors. Public relations, curatorial, schools, controller, maintenance and security personnel reported to him beginning in November. The institute had begun using established business practices, and visitation totaled 500,000 for the year.

However, Ulbrich's brief tenure was stormy. Ablewhite, who now held the title of chief curator, fought for and won autonomy in collection-related areas. Thus Ulbrich operated basically as a business manager. Ablewhite, in fact, was asked by trustee B. J. Craig to take over village operations immediately after Mrs. Ford's death. Although Ray Dahlinger left shortly after, administrative confusion governed the next few months.

In January of 1951, A. K. Mills assumed the new post of executive director, which finally gave one person definite lines of authority on paper *and* in practice over both the village and museum. The general manager's position was soon abolished. More positive moves included hiring additional professional staff members at a measured pace, a practice that would continue with growing attendance and expanding programs.

An American music display initiated special exhibitions in 1951. Of others that followed in the next two years, the most significant was the 1953 permanent installation of "Henry Ford — A Personal History" on the second floor of the museum's Independence Hall section. The exhibit helped mark the Ford Motor Company's 50th anniversary. That year also saw the official name change from The Edison Institute Museum to The Henry Ford Museum, the opening of the Ford Homestead to the public, and the Ford Motor Company's gift of the Dearborn Inn to the institute. This hotel, located near the village and museum, was one of the first constructed specifically to serve airline passengers.

Although the museum made few significant additions to the collections during these years of transition, the trustees did authorize the sale of surplus artifacts with the proviso that the income be used to buy other, more important pieces.

New one- and two-day events and historical re-enactments served to involve the public more actively in the institute's resources. The first three of these—Country Fair, Old Car Festival and the Famous Early Movies Series—increased in popularity through the next two decades.

Physical changes between 1947 and 1954 were minor. Construction of both a Quonset hut for village service operations and a serpentine brick wall around the Ford Motor Company's test track, however, indicated the growing separation between institute and motor company operations.

1948-1954

With the arrival of new staff and methods, the old ways and indecisiveness that lingered after Henry Ford's death gradually faded. By the fall of 1952, only the kindergarten through sixth grade classes remained of the village schools. The trustees in 1953 approved the concept of redesigning the museum's mechanical arts hall. Perhaps most symbolically, institute officials in 1954 added the first building to Ford's beloved village since his death: the H. J. Heinz House from Pittsburgh.

Fresh approaches to the fulfillment of Henry Ford's educational goals beckoned on the horizon. An exciting period of burgeoning programs and collection refinement lay ahead.

1

2

New faces began to mingle with the old as an organized line
of authority evolved in the early 1950s. Benson Ford (1, right,
accepting the millionth Dayton bicycle for the museum in
1947) became President of The Edison Institute Board of
Trustees shortly after his grandfather's death in April 1947. He
remained in that position until his younger brother, William
Clay Ford (2, at Henry Ford's Highland Park office desk,
1953), assumed the title in April 1951.

126

6

10

Hayward S. Ablewhite (3) moved from the Ford Motor Company's Sociological Department into the post of Edison Institute Museum director on February 1, 1949. Fred Smith (4, right, accepting the millionth Bendix washing machine in the museum, October 1947) had directed daily museum operations since the mid-1930s. Shortly after Ablewhite's arrival, Smith became ill and left the institute.

Edison Institute general manager since 1949, Emil A. Ulbrich (5) saw his position abolished after A. K. Mills (6) became executive director on January 5, 1951. Mills served simultaneously as director of the newly established Ford Archives, housed in Fair Lane. Ablewhite shifted to the position of chief curator and later to director of Public Relations. Creation of the executive director's position, coupled with Ray Dahlinger's departure the previous fall, solidified joint leadership of village and museum operations, which had split after Henry Ford's stroke in 1945. Dahlinger had controlled village operations from 1947 to 1950, reporting directly to Clara Ford.

Under Mills, the staff formed which would guide the complex through the next two decades. In the spring of 1952, Frank Caddy (7) became director of administration, a newly created position. Caddy came to the institute in 1931 through the Henry Ford Trade School and joined the permanent staff the next year. In 1940, he entered the Payroll and Accounts Payable Department, formed in 1938. That office, growing more autonomous as it severed motor company and Ford Foundation connections, provided the only staff serving both museum and village operations from 1947 to 1951. Named controller in 1945, Caddy became treasurer to the board of trustees in 1951. He would remain a guiding force in institute operations through the 1970s.

Ray Cline (8) replaced Caddy as controller. Cline worked at the institute for about a year before World War II, then rejoined the staff in 1947.

Gustav Munchow (9), a supervisory member of the village grounds crew as early as 1930, took charge of village and museum maintenance upon Dahlinger's departure.

In February 1952, Mills appointed as curator of fine arts the man who would eventually succeed him, Donald A. Shelley (10). The future executive director's affiliation with other museums spanned 17 years.

11   12   13

Clara Bryant Ford (11), last of The Edison Institute's three founders, died on September 29, 1950. A constant supporter of her husband during the building of the village and museum, Clara watched over the complex after Henry's illness in 1945. At his death, direction of the organization fell on her shoulders, and, for the next several years, she maintained it the way she felt Henry would have. Her estate left the institute a $9 million endowment.

Living a long and rich life, Clara remained close to her family (12, with Edsel when she was about 27 years of age, c. 1893). Her rural background, evident in her deep love of flowers and gardens, never left her (13, in the late 1930s in her extensive gardens at Fair Lane). To Henry, she was his "believer" throughout their life together. She shared his abiding interest in Greenfield Village, where they frequently walked together in the twilight hours, enjoying the comfortable atmosphere of the past (14).

128

14

15

Of the relatively few collection items acquired during the transitional years, three stand out: a 1939 Lincoln limousine used by Presidents Roosevelt and Truman (15); the Charles Brady King collection of miniature steam engines (16, Hayward Ablewhite, left, examining an engine with Charles Brady King); and a bronze statue of Thomas Edison cast by James Earle Fraser. Henry Ford commissioned the last-named work in 1930, but the war years and a bronze shortage delayed completion until 1949, when the statue found a home in the museum. In 1953, it was moved to the Menlo Park Compound in the village (17 and 18).

17

18

16

19

20

Through special exhibits, the new staff began to interpret
Henry Ford's amassed treasures for the public. One of the first
exhibits, staged in 1951, featured American music (19,
William Distin, museum librarian, standing, and Hayward
Ablewhite with early music manuscripts). The museum
also inaugurated its annual Antiques Lecture Series in 1951,
featuring many of the country's decorative arts experts.

Beginning in May 1952, museum collections came to
America's hometowns when a traveling exhibit, "Industrial
Progress, U.S.A.," hit the road for a three-year, nationwide
tour. The 30-foot trailer carrying the display contained 200
years of American achievements in such areas as fashion,
automobiles, housewares, heating, plumbing and electronics
(20, new executive director Donald Shelley and Hayward
Ablewhite greeting truck driver and exhibitor Carl
Malotka on his return to the museum in June 1955).
During the summer months, the museum often housed the
traveling exhibit.

Several special exhibits highlighted the 1953 season. "Sports
Cars in Review," launched that year, annually drew large
crowds for 25 years (21, a 1935 Bentley at the second year's
show, entitled "Sports Cars Unlimited"). The museum
staff also installed "American Indian Culture" that year (22).
On loan from the Sheedy collection, previously in storage for
half a century, the display stood for six years.

21

22

1953 also marked the 50th anniversary of the Ford Motor Company. In conjunction with that observance, an exhibit honoring the life of the company's and institute's founder, Henry Ford, was conceived by his grandsons and constructed on the second floor of the museum's Independence Hall replica. The Ford Archives staff and the institute's new professional staff selected and arranged the artifacts and documents in the rooms which 24 years earlier had hosted a reception for Light's Golden Jubilee banquet guests.

Installation of the permanent exhibit – the largest since the museum's opening – constituted a major project. The size of some objects presented problems. The 15 millionth Model T Ford, made in 1927, journeyed to the second floor without too much trouble (23). However, reminiscent of the 1896 Quadricycle that was too large to fit through the doorway in Henry's 58 Bagley Avenue shed, the 1927 "T" demanded maneuvering through the last portal (24). Employees previewed "Henry Ford: A Personal History" on May 7 (25, gathered around Ford's first gasoline engine, left to right: Frank Caddy, Hayward Ablewhite, Marge Caddy, Katharine Bryant Hagler, the first member of the professional staff Ablewhite hired, decorative arts curator Gerald Gibson and the William Distins).

23

24

26

Village special events, one- or two-day festivals illustrating aspects of American history through the use of artifacts, began in 1951. The first event, Country Fair of Yesteryear, revived the May festival formerly staged by the village schoolchildren. The youngsters were back in featured roles, rolling hoops (26) and dancing around the Maypole in the updated show, while the overhauled Suwanee provided the backdrop to an old-fashioned minstrel show (27).

During the early fall of 1951, the Old Car Festival, destined to become an annual favorite, convened on the village green. Eighty-eight cars participated in the first event, causing a few friendly "traffic jams" (28).

That same year, on the 175th anniversary of the signing of the Declaration of Independence, Nebraska Senator Kenneth S. Wherry spoke at a reenactment in front of the museum's Independence Hall entrance. The ceremony in later years would become an annual event. Also in 1951, showings of Great Films of the Century began in the museum theater, to the delight of silver screen fans.

Most changes in the village seemed relatively minor during the first seven years after Henry Ford's death. The redecorated Clinton Inn cafeteria opened to the public for meal service in 1951. Except for one brief period in the early 1930s, it had served only village schoolchildren.

28

27

29

30

After ten years of winter hibernation, the village resumed year-round operations in 1951 (29, Plymouth House, once Ed Cutler's office, which became an antiques and crafts sales shop in 1953). Visitors could now enjoy the atmosphere of an old American town during all four seasons.

An eight-foot-high serpentine brick wall, built by the Ford Motor Company in 1952 to separate the Ford Test Track from Village Road (30), signified the growing autonomy of Edison Institute operations. Occasionally, however, the two entities joined forces. During pace car preparations for the 1953 Indianapolis 500, for example, the museum staff put "999," Henry Ford's old racer, in working order, running it close to 60 mph on the Ford Test Track (31, William Clay Ford test driving the official pace car, a 1953 Ford later placed in the museum's transportation collection alongside "999").

The Ford Homestead, the last building Henry Ford moved to the village, opened to the public on April 1, 1953, as part of the Ford Motor Company's 50th anniversary celebrations.

133

31

33

32

The one notable addition to the village scene between 1947 and 1954 was the 1854 H. J. Heinz House from Sharpsburg, Pennsylvania. The building served as the Heinz family home for 15 years before it became the first Heinz factory. By 1875 the company had moved to Pittsburgh. After the building floated five miles down the Allegheny River to the Heinz plant in 1904 (32), it functioned as the company museum. In 1953, the expanding firm donated the house to Greenfield Village, and disassembly began that fall (33).

By late spring of 1954, the first historic structure to be added to the village since 1944 lacked only landscaping and painting (34). The restored interior displayed some of the 57 varieties that made Heinz famous (35). Dedication ceremonies followed on June 16, 1954.

35

34

After 18 years of operation, The Edison Institute High School closed its doors following June graduation ceremonies in 1952 (36, graduates in the museum theater). Kindergarten through sixth grade classes still met in their various village locations. Parts of the Recreation Building, which housed high school classes after The Edison Institute of Technology closed in 1943, served the remaining primary grades and community groups. Starting in 1953, upstairs dormitories provided overnight accommodations for visiting school groups. The Henry Ford Trade School ceased operation in 1952 as well, after graduating more than 8,000 boys.

The year 1954 marked The Edison Institute's 25th anniversary and the Diamond Jubilee of Light. A number of special activities, including the dedication of the Heinz House, commemorated the first quarter century of village and museum activity.

While preventive maintenance and work on crafts buildings continued, the village's industrial area opened to visitors for the first time since the early 1930s. In the museum, the Garden Room Restaurant, with an adjacent terrace, started serving meals.

The museum's major anniversary exhibit, "The Light We Live By," featured old illuminating devices and important developments in lighting history. October 21 ceremonies included a visit to Menlo Park by William Clay Ford and John Edison Sloane, a descendant of Thomas Edison (37), and a banquet in Lovett Hall attended by a distinguished group of nearly 400 people.

1955-1969

Many people seem to believe that Greenfield Village and The Edison Institute and Museum at Dearborn, with their specimens of an earlier type of American life and industry, are just a kind of antiquarian hobby of mine. I do not deny that they have given me a great deal of interest and pleasure. But the project is vastly more than a hobby. It has very definite purposes, and I hope will have results lasting down the years. One purpose is to remind the public . . . how far and how fast we have come in technical progress in the last century or so. If we have come so far and so fast, is it likely that we shall stop now?

— HENRY FORD

Chapter Six

Stability Fosters Growth

I would like to take this opportunity to thank all our employees who responded so well in making our TV shows such a success. . . . I am sure that you will all agree we can be very proud of the way Greenfield Village and the Henry Ford Museum were represented in this national TV show. . . . Thanks to your efforts, 16 million Americans were able to pay a brief "visit" to Greenfield Village on October 25.
Donald A. Shelley, message to employees in The Greenfield Villager, *November 1, 1955*

On October 25, 1955, the National Broadcasting Company televised three live, remote color programs from Greenfield Village. The day proved significant in a number of ways. Television technology showed off its growing versatility, and the institute realized both the benefits of national exposure and the importance of employee participation in the operation of the complex. These programs symbolized the outward thrust and inward examination the next 15 years would bring.

Employees enjoyed significant benefits by 1955. Improvements included better health care insurance, a pension plan, the transfer of all permanent hourly employees to a salary pay schedule, an employee lunch program, discounts on sales items, a recreation program and yearly family picnics.

In addition to the high employee morale, top management positions had stabilized with William Clay Ford as president of the board of trustees and Donald A. Shelley as executive director. The establishment of directorships of administration, education and crafts strengthened formerly diffuse operations.

Shelley, who had served as curator of fine arts since 1952, replaced A. K. Mills, who died of a heart attack in the fall of 1954. Mills had led the institute through several rough years. Shelley would achieve stability and national recognition for the quality of the institute's holdings and educational potential.

Perhaps best known for his development of the museum's decorative arts collection, Shelley directed a program aimed at refining all collection areas. Steps included research, examination of objects, analysis of the bounds of each specific collection, addition of items to fill gaps and acquisition of unique artifacts. This shaping process would continue through the 1960s and into the 1970s.

The most significant acquisition of the period, and certainly one of the most important in the entire history of the institute, was the Ford Motor Company's 1964 gift of the Ford Archives. Received on the 35th anniversary of The Edison Institute, the archives contain millions of documents and photographs related to the life and work of Henry Ford. They also include transcripts of more than 300 oral reminiscences by those who knew Henry Ford personally and professionally.

Beginning in 1955 the institute conducted an oral history program of its own. An archives committee interviewed several people associated with the building of the village and museum.

Even while the staff examined and strengthened collections, the public was demanding more and more attention as the institute fought to become self-supporting. The expanded Education Building dormitories could now accommodate 90 students from visiting school groups. New eating facilities opened in the village and museum, village buildings festooned with decorations heralded the Christmas season and the cider mill began public operation. Thirty-four repainted buildings joined several refurbished and newly opened ones to give the village added appeal.

1955-1969

The museum kept pace with the village, as curators installed as many as six special exhibitions a year. In 1952, the institute launched the first of three nationwide traveling exhibits, "Industrial Progress U.S.A.," which in three years visited all United States cities with populations over 100,000.

Five special events, which became annual affairs for the public, were created between 1955 and 1969. Extensive television coverage and the production of several films on the village served to increase national visibility. Attendance rose dramatically, climbing from 500,000 in 1950 to 1 million in 1960. By 1969, visitation surpassed 1.3 million yearly.

The village and museum were clearly a national attraction. The solidified and seasoned staff continually upgraded the collections. Despite the public's growing awareness of the complex, however, concern was rising over what the visitors experienced on site. Two major moves in 1969 demonstrated the administration's desire for improvement in this area.

The last of the village schools closed as the rising costs of this unique learning experience were not justified for such a small number of students. The newly established Adult Education and School Services departments sought wider participation in educational programs.

And, on the 40th anniversary of the institute's founding, board chairman William Clay Ford announced a $40-million, long-range development program that was to have a tremendous impact on visitor involvement with Henry Ford's bank of historical resources. America's heritage was guaranteed a long life.

The magic word in the mid-1950s was "television!" The first program broadcast from the village, Dave Garroway's "Today" show on April 18, 1955, featured carriages and antique cars from museum collections. The institute also initiated its own show, "Window to the Past," in the fall of 1955 when Detroit's educational station, WTVS, Channel 56, began operation. Aimed at children of elementary school age, the 15-minute telecast presented flashbacks showing life a hundred years earlier (1, "Toys of Yesteryear" segment with institute hostess Marion Corwell).

The big day, however, dawned on October 25, 1955. The village green resembled a large set as NBC-TV crews scurried to cover three different programs (2). The "Today" show was back, beaming chapel services to viewers in three time zones. Video tape was not available, and the program had to be performed live three times. During mid-morning, a typical day in a mid-19th-century American village was portrayed on Arlene Francis' "Home" show. Action took place on the green and inside several village buildings. The "Howdy Doody Show" aired during the afternoon from the Scotch Settlement School. Village schoolchildren combined with the professional

cast (3) to demonstrate differences between school days in 1855 and 1955. More than 50 institute employees performed throughout the day, while at least that many more worked behind the scenes to put the buildings, grounds and actors in accurate period appearance.

Village settings and resources were still desirable a decade later as the ABC network based the last of its "Discovery" series there in 1967.

Special events thrived during the 1950s and 1960s. The annual Muzzle Loaders' Festival began as the Greenfield Village Turkey Shoot in November 1955. Held on the open field behind South Dearborn Road (4), the festival soon drew hundreds of participants.

The Midwest Antiques Forum debuted in 1960 with a five-day program concentrating on "Collecting Americana." The accompanying exhibit, "Americana: Midwest Collectors' Choice," displayed more than 1,000 examples of the decorative arts owned by 80 private collectors.

Other new events included a ten-day Famous Early Movie Festival in 1961, a revamping of the Great Films of the Century program of a decade earlier. Lectures, nature walks, workshops and garden tours highlighted the first annual Clara B. Ford Garden Forum in 1962, while re-creations of classic early American plays, staged in the museum theater in 1964, initiated the American Drama Festival.

Two earlier events, Country Fair and Old Car Festival, continued in expanded formats. The 1958 Old Car Festival (5) surpassed the largest single-day crowd in the institute's history, attracting 14,611 visitors. The same festival would set a new record in 1972 with 24,262 admissions. Fourth of July observances became an annual event after Michigan Governor George Romney spoke in 1964 at "Let Freedom Ring" ceremonies at the museum entrance (6).

7   8

Throughout the 1950s, refurbishing began on dozens of village buildings, particularly the historic homes. For many, 20 years or more had passed since their original restorations. Work included interior and exterior painting, decorating with more authentic pieces and the opening of rooms and entire houses previously closed to the public. The Webster House (7, "before" and 8, "after" refurbishing views of Webster's upstairs study) exemplified the last category, having served as a school building for most of its existence at Greenfield Village.

Two new buildings of note were added to the village between 1958 and 1963. Both had connections with former village architect Ed Cutler. Called back from retirement for consultation, Cutler first participated in an oral reminiscence program designed to preserve some of the institute's early history. An archives committee was established for this purpose in 1955 and Cutler was one of the first persons interviewed (9, Cutler, holding a microphone, discussing the construction of the Menlo Park Lab with members of the archives committee, left to right: librarian Ken Metcalf, audio-visual coordinator Dave Glick, decorative arts curator George Bird, and custodian and interpreter of the Menlo Park complex Charles Natzel).

9

10

11

12

In the village, Cutler designed a new lunch stand, completed in 1958, and supervised the disassembly of the second historic building added since Henry Ford's death: Dr. Alonson B. Howard's 1839 office from Calhoun County, Michigan. In 1855 young Dr. Howard took possession of the small building, originally a one-room school, and partitioned it into a waiting room, office and laboratory. At his death in 1883, his wife shipped the contents to their son, also a physician, and padlocked the door. Howard's great-grandson presented the building, with all its original furnishings, to the institute.

The dismantling of this country doctor's office enabled the new generation of museum administrators to see the almost legendary Cutler in action. After making preliminary sketches of the building on its original site (10, with chief curator Minor Wine Thomas, left, and Executive Director Donald Shelley, right) and numbering the critical construction elements (11), he took additional notes and measurements as the building came down. Cutler's detailed drawings of the structure, made during 1959 and 1960, would help in the reconstruction. The restored building was dedicated on October 15, 1963.

Village crafts expanded under Shelley, including hooked rug pattern-making from 100-year-old stencils. In 1959 the museum acquired 750 original rug stencils made by Edward Sands Frost and demonstrated their use in the Cotton Gin Mill (12).

143

The forces of nature have not always been kind to Henry Ford's typical American village. Indeed, the village would not be typical if fire, flood, wind and other natural tragedies never struck. One of the first catastrophes was a 1954 fire in a village barn, which caused moderate damage to the structure and the death of a number of horses. Another fire destroyed a small barn, part of a children's miniature farm between South Dearborn Road and the Menlo Park complex, in 1958 (13).

Probably the most disastrous occurrence in institute history, a museum fire in 1970 ruined a number of collection items. Several structures along the Street of Early American Shops also went up in smoke (14). Despite the extensive damage, which was considerably minimized by an alert staff, the museum remained closed to the public for only two days.

16

A Rouge River flood in June 1968 nearly destroyed an old friend of Henry Ford and the village schoolchildren – the steamer Suwanee (15). Since its original construction by Conrad Menge in 1929-30, the Suwanee had endured several overhauls, including the installation of a new boiler in 1954 (16). The 1968 flood waters seriously damaged her hull and parts of her decks. Down but not out, the boat underwent reconstruction in 1969. The new wooden hull arrived at the village lagoon via truck later that year, taking its latest "first" run in May 1970 (17).

17

18

Two museum traveling exhibits followed the successful
"Industrial Progress U.S.A." in the early 1950s. "Schoolroom
Progress U.S.A.," focusing on educational advances since the
days of the one-room school, hit the rails in 1955 after the
official dedication of the two cars in Washington, D.C. (18).

The institute also displayed its third exhibit on wheels,
"Main Street U.S.A.," in railroad cars. Following its
conception in early 1959 (19) came roughing in on the museum
floor in December, the installation of exhibits and, finally,
dedication ceremonies at Smiths Creek Station on April 23,
1960 (20). Designed by consultant Ed Cutler, the early
American shops arranged on one side of the two cars faced
modern settings on the other side. Like "Schoolroom Progress,"
"Main Street" traveled the country's rails for five years.

In the museum itself, the physical layout for the period
1955-69 was set (21). In the main exhibition hall, special

19

20

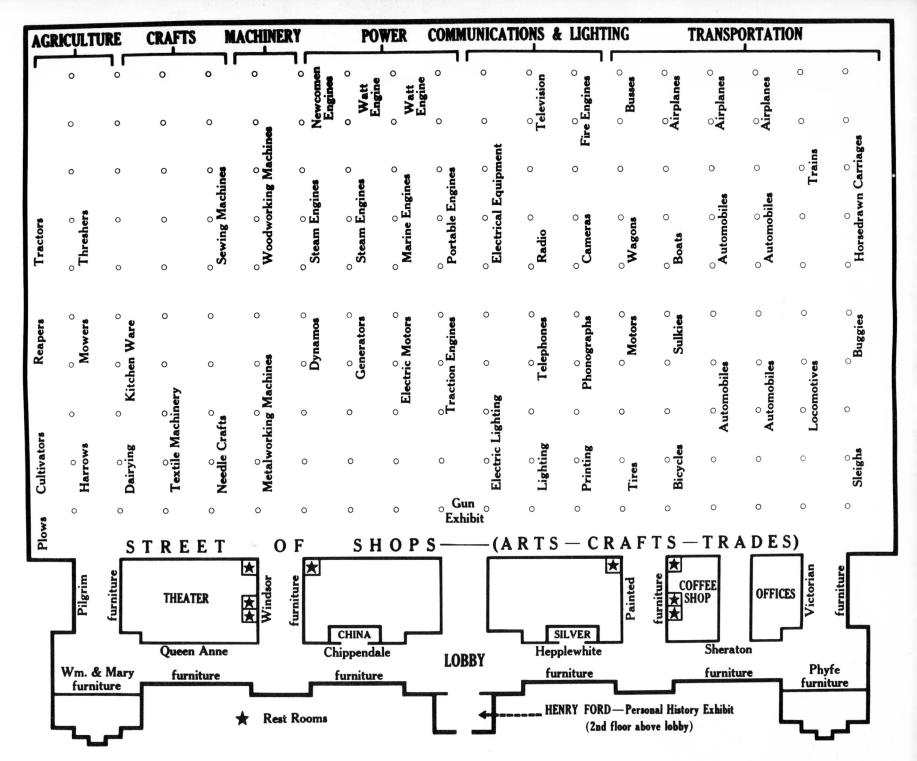

AGRICULTURE   CRAFTS   MACHINERY   POWER   COMMUNICATIONS & LIGHTING   TRANSPORTATION

Newcomen Engines · Watt Engine · Watt Engine · Television · Fire Engines · Busses · Airplanes · Airplanes · Airplanes

Sewing Machines · Woodworking Machines · Steam Engines · Steam Engines · Marine Engines · Portable Engines · Electrical Equipment · Radio · Cameras · Wagons · Boats · Automobiles · Automobiles · Trains · Horsedrawn Carriages

Tractors · Threshers

Reapers · Mowers · Kitchen Ware · Dynamos · Generators · Electric Motors · Traction Engines · Telephones · Phonographs · Motors · Sulkies · Buggies

Cultivators · Harrows · Dairying · Textile Machinery · Needle Crafts · Metalworking Machines · Electric Lighting · Lighting · Printing · Tires · Bicycles · Automobiles · Automobiles · Locomotives · Sleighs

Electric Lighting · Automobiles · Automobiles · Locomotives

Plows

Gun Exhibit

STREET OF SHOPS ——— (ARTS — CRAFTS — TRADES)

Pilgrim furniture

THEATER — Queen Anne — Windsor furniture

★

CHINA — Chippendale furniture

★

SILVER — Hepplewhite furniture — Painted furniture

COFFEE SHOP — Sheraton furniture ★ ★

OFFICES — Victorian furniture — Phyfe furniture

Wm. & Mary furniture

LOBBY

★ Rest Rooms

← HENRY FORD — *Personal History Exhibit*
(2nd floor above lobby)

21

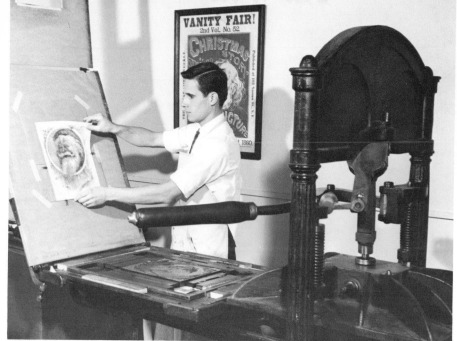

26

25

29

shows occupied the reserved area beyond the Street of Shops. Among them were: "Home for Christmas, 1958 (22); "Crafts at Christmas," 1962 (23); and "The World in Miniature," 1963, featuring a scale model of the Fords' Richmond Hill, Georgia, residence (24) which Clara ordered built so that she could decorate the rooms on a manageable scale before actual furnishing.

The 15-year period from 1955 to 1969 also witnessed significant additions to the decorative arts and other collection areas, including:

(25) A six-paneled silver drinking bowl, 1699, made by New Yorker Jesse Kip—the earliest known American racing trophy retaining its original form.

(26) A high-backed, Chippendale mahogany armchair made in Philadelphia by Thomas Affleck, c. 1794, to function as the speaker's chair in Congress Hall's Supreme Court Chamber.

(27) A c. 1922 Super Heterodyne Radio invented and built by Edwin Armstrong—the first self-contained portable radio.

(28) A cast-iron, six-plate stove, c. 1760, made at Hampton Furnace, Frederick County, Maryland.

(29) An inlaid silver Kentucky-type rifle, c. 1830, made by G. Scott of Coshocton, Ohio.

(30) A Bugatti "Royale," 1930, one of only six engines and chassis built by famed French race car designer Ettore Bugatti to be fitted with custom-built bodies.

28

27

30

149

One of the largest, and certainly most photographed, exhibits in the museum arrived in 1956 and almost did not make it inside! In July of that year, the C & O Railway presented the museum with a 600-ton Allegheny locomotive, built in 1941 and representing the developmental peak of coal-burning engines. Despite removal of parts of the engine prior to attempts to squeeze it through one of the huge back doors of the museum, the fit was tight. When it took the wrong fork in the tracks, it scraped the side of the door. On September 1, the crew tried again, first greasing the tracks to enable the locomotive to negotiate the severe turn into the museum (31). On the third attempt, "Big Al" finally – though barely – made it (32), easing into its spot next to several earlier steam-driven trains (33).

In 1964, the vast Ford Archives – a collection of millions of documents, photographs and memorabilia related to the personal and professional lives of Henry Ford and his family – came to The Edison Institute as a gift of the Ford Motor Company. This voluminous collection, said to be the most complete business archives in existence (34, pre-1970 collection of books whose authors drew from Ford Archives resources), added tremendous educational value to the museum's existing library and archival holdings.

31

32

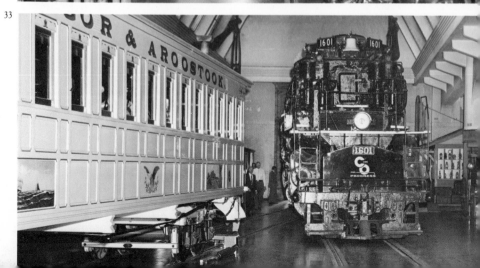

33

34

The 1960s presented a mixture of endings and beginnings for The Edison Institute. In 1961, the two architects, Ed Cutler and Robert O. Derrick, died.

The last vestige of the village school system — the elementary grades — closed in 1969, 40 years after its inception under Henry Ford's watchful eye (35, the last graduating class). Just as this program terminated, however, the institute attempted to open its educational resources to more people with the creation of two new departments, School Services and Adult Education. The latter's craft and enrichment courses and School Services' coordinating efforts met with immediate success. Rarely a night went by when the expanded dormitories in Lovett Hall were not filled.

Another milestone was the transfer in 1955 of all permanent hourly employees to a salary basis (36, hourly employees punching out in the village garage for the last time, November 1955).

Guests at the 40th anniversary ceremonies on October 21, 1969, toured two museum exhibits in addition to attending ceremonies at the Menlo Park Laboratory and a banquet in Lovett Hall. The two exhibits, "Treasures of the Henry Ford Museum" and "Decorative Arts Accessions: A Decade and a Half of Collecting," focused on both the depth of Henry Ford's collections and the intensive strengthening of those collections during the previous 15 years. The 40th anniversary celebration demonstrated the establishment of a solid foundation of presentation techniques and special events.

The announcement on October 21, 1969, by William Clay Ford of a multi-million dollar expansion and development program, however, would encourage the institute staff to extend beyond the base of the past and build for the future.

35

36

1970-1979

*We have only started on our development
of our country—we have not as yet, with
all our talk of wonderful progress, done
more than scratch the surface. The
progress has been wonderful enough—but
when we compare what we have done with
what there is to do, then our past
accomplishments are as nothing....*

—HENRY FORD

152

Chapter Seven

Giving the Past a Future

I think the institute is one of the great philanthropic legacies of my grandfather. It in no way diminishes the significance of this historic resource to note that he underestimated its financial needs when he conceived it more than a generation ago.

He predicted then that it might some day accommodate as many as 300,000 visitors annually. Last year, more than 1.3 million visitors passed through our gates.

William Clay Ford, 40th Anniversary Address, October 21, 1969

In announcing $20 million capital improvement and endowment grants from both the Ford Foundation and the Ford Motor Company Fund, William Clay Ford stressed that the institute would be embarking "on a development program far more ambitious than any it has undertaken since its inception."

The board of trustees recognized the necessity of a financial shot in the arm, not only to provide adequate maintenance of existing facilities but to inaugurate more progressive interpretation and education programs. "The enormous increase in attendance and the evolution of the institute as a diverse educational and cultural center have consumed earlier gifts, and it is only through these new funds that the achievements and momentum of the past can be preserved," Ford said.

The staff wasted little time launching a capital improvements program, particularly in Greenfield Village. Some repairs and maintenance were underway even before the announcement. Service facilities, such as sidewalks, restaurants, restrooms, orientation centers and giftshops were either upgraded or constructed. Two large-scale projects — the construction and equipping of a perimeter railroad and the creation of a turn-of-the-century amusement park — reached completion in 1974. A multi-building crafts center was erected the following year and, in 1976 and 1977, workers finished renovation of select industrial buildings.

Major additions of historic structures continued with the moving and reconstruction of an early-18th-century saltbox house from Andover, Connecticut. This building, opened to the public in 1978, filled an important gap in the village's three-dimensional chronology of American house development.

The museum received similar attention with the installation of new fire protection systems, two years after a 1970 fire tragically pointed out the vital need for such equipment. Significant additions within the 14-acre building included a preservation and conservation laboratory, a photographic studio and two new collections galleries. A new giftshop and a large cafeteria and restaurant also opened.

New administrators filled more clearly defined lines of authority. William Clay Ford assumed the newly designated position of chairman of the board of trustees in 1968. That same year, Shelley was appointed president and the title of executive director was abolished. In 1976, Frank Caddy, employed by the institute since 1931, took over the presidential reins from retiring Shelley. Caddy, a strong force in the administration since the early 1950s, quickly moved the development program forward with the assistance of an able staff. Vice-presidencies were created in the areas of collections and presentation, corporate services and public affairs. The 1978 addition of a vice-presidency of education reflected renewed commitment to Henry Ford's original purpose in creating the institute: using the institute's resources to convey the nation's heritage to the American public.

Presentation of special exhibits and special events continued (particularly during the nation's Bicentennial), while virtually all areas of museum operation improved significantly in scope and quality during the 1970s. A museum membership program, launched in 1971, numbered close to 9,000 individuals, families and corporations by 1979. The contributions and support of The Friends of Greenfield Village and Henry Ford Museum have become vital to the institute's development.

1970-1979

The collections themselves received extensive evaluation between 1976 and 1979 in terms of their use for general educational purposes. Henry Ford believed everything he collected should be displayed. He felt people could learn by studying minute improvements in the progression of technology. Museum curators of the late 1970s removed duplicate and near-duplicate artifacts from exhibit and placed them in study collections.

A total redesign of the museum's eight-acre mechanical arts hall (renamed the Hall of Technology) resulted. Displaying the most representative artifacts and explaining them in an easily understood system of labels and graphics would help the public comprehend the intertwining story of American technological growth. June 1979 marked the completion of the Hall of Technology project, with the installation of a 30,000-square-foot Interpretive Center. This introductory exhibit presents a three-dimensional and graphic overview of American industrial progress. Redesigning the old mechanical arts exhibits marked the largest reinstallation ever attempted in an existing museum building.

Henry Ford made his greatest contribution to America's heritage with his incredible construction project, undertaken from 1927 to 1947. During that 20-year span he built a home for America's past and furnished it with the artifacts of our ancestors' day-to-day lives. Ford succinctly stated his purpose in founding The Edison Institute:

> When we are through, we shall have reproduced American life as lived; and that, I think, is the best way of preserving at least a part of our history and tradition. For by looking at things people used and that show the way they lived, a better and truer impression can be gained than could be had in a month of reading — even if there were books whose authors had the facilities to discover the minute details of the older life.

The key phrase in Ford's statement of purpose is "when we are through." The further and faster the human race goes, the more difficult it becomes to remember its receding and ever-expanding past. And because historical institutions shoulder the responsibility of presenting and interpreting tangible, three-dimensional fragments of the past, the job will never be "through." Each year produces more material for yet another chapter of human history.

Henry Ford's descendants have continued his ideal of keeping the American story vital to today's and tomorrow's generations. A statement by his grandson, institute board chairman William Clay Ford, perhaps best summarizes this commitment: "One of America's strengths is its heritage. To neglect that heritage is to risk a future in which our young people in particular will find themselves without a means of building on the firm and reassuring foundation of the past."

America's rich heritage found a home in Greenfield Village and Henry Ford Museum. Henry Ford, a man who had the courage to attempt and the power to realize his dream, built the sturdy foundation. It is up to this and succeeding generations to keep this home in good repair.

Throughout the 1960s and 1970s, The Edison Institute's staff grew in number, leveling off at about 350 full-time, salaried employees. As programs and staff expanded, so did the management organization that would direct them. By the nation's Bicentennial year, the people who would guide the institute through its most exciting period since the pre-dedication building programs were on the scene.

At the top, William Clay Ford (1) was elected to the new post of chairman of the board of trustees in 1968. Donald A. Shelley subsequently became president of the institute and a trustee. Frank Caddy, director of administration, was named vice-president of administration and a trustee in the same year. The year 1976 marked Shelley's retirement and Caddy's appointment as president (2, Shelley, left, and Caddy at Shelley's August 1976 retirement luncheon in Lovett Hall).

Robert G. Wheeler, director of crafts for the institute since 1967 (3), joined Caddy as a vice-president and trustee in 1969, with responsibilities for research and interpretation. In the major realignment of 1976, his area of responsibility shifted to collections and presentation.

The board named two other vice-presidents and trustees in 1976: George Johnson (4) moved from director of Grounds and Buildings to vice-president of corporate services; and J. Robert Dawson (5) rose from director of Public Relations to vice-president of public affairs. Ray Cline (6) assumed the post of treasurer in 1976, after serving eight years as assistant treasurer.

In December 1978, the Department of Education expanded to form a separate division within the institute, with the appointment of David T. Glick (7), previously director of education, as vice-president and trustee. Concurrently, two new trustees were elected: Lynn Ford Alandt (8) and Sheila Firestone Ford (9), representing the fourth generation of Fords to direct the destinies of America's heritage.

By 1979 the board of trustees included, in addition to the above-named members: Henry Ford II (10), since 1943; Edith McNaughton Ford (11), since 1971; and Walter Buhl Ford (12), since 1971.

156

1

3

2

 4

 5

 7

 6

 8

 9

 10

 11

 12

157

One of the first additions to the village under the development program announced in 1969 was a perimeter railroad. Henry Ford's active interest in railroads, a vital segment of 19th-century American life, surfaced in both his idea of a roundhouse for the museum and his frequent runs on the Rocket and the President. The two growth patterns found in the traditional American town—the establishment of the village green and the development of industry around the railroad—were thus joined in Greenfield Village.

To have something to run on the proposed rails, the institute staff located an 1873 Mason-Fairlie locomotive in Michigan's Upper Peninsula mining country. The 36-ton, steam-driven locomotive, called the Torch Lake, was a gift of Universal Oil Products Company.

A rather bleak view from the Torch Lake's shed at the Ahmeek Mine near Calumet, Michigan, greeted institute officials arriving to oversee the engine's transport to Greenfield Village (13). A crew hauled the engine with attached tender from the shed and up a ramp onto a flatcar since it would not make the trip under its own power. Nine days later, the Torch Lake sat on the village siding next to Smiths Creek Station.

Until the installation of the perimeter tracks, the Torch Lake carried visitors up and down the siding between Smiths Creek and the Michigan Central tracks. By June 1972, the village tracks were laid and the train was making test runs. Donald Shelley and William Clay Ford drove in the golden spikes in August (14) and the Torch Lake took three carloads of visitors on a memorable inaugural run (15).

The next year, an 1868 Mason-American type locomotive from the limestone mines of Thomas Edison's New Jersey cement company joined the Torch Lake in village service.

16

A year after the Torch Lake's 1972 inaugural run, construction began on Main Street Station, located between the village gatehouse and the Village Print Shop (16). At the other end of the village, on the banks of the Suwanee Lagoon, another station was planned in conjunction with the construction of a new village area—a turn-of-the-century amusement park.

The Suwanee Park Project (17, left to right: bandstand, lagoon, railroad station in distance, ice cream parlor, Tin Lantern Giftshop and penny arcade building, and Riverfront Restaurant) neared completion by May 1974. Furnishings for the ice cream parlor came from the 1870 Clark Drugstore in Natick, Massachusetts. The penny arcade housed 32 original 1898-1932 machines. Other amusements included a c. 1913 Herschell-Spillman carousel (18, during construction), a raft ride to Suwanee Island and, of course, excursions on the Suwanee herself. The riverfront park, neatly nestled between the Suwanee Lagoon, the old Rouge River bed and the rear of residential row, flourished by mid-summer (19) as clearly a "hands-on" historical experience (20).

17

18

19

21

22

As with most of the village buildings, the authentic elements of the Suwanee Park project needed restoration. The institute's Conservation Department painstakingly returned the carousel animals to their original appearances (21) before the area opened to the public.

The development program provided for such visitor amenities as new brick sidewalks and benches in 1972. The year 1973 brought a remodeled and enlarged gatehouse (22, addition under construction at right) and an extensive village book and souvenir shop occupying a series of colonial styled buildings (22, left). Also in that year, a new lunch stand, the Pond 'n' Coop, went up near the Ackley Covered Bridge as did new restrooms.

Other village and grounds improvements during the 1970s included the renovation of selected industrial buildings and the repair of numerous other structures. Flood protection and sanitary sewer systems were installed, parking lots were improved and enlarged, and a 22,500 square-foot storage building was constructed behind the museum.

The crafts center expanded in 1975 (23) with the construction of a bakery and a barn to house pottery, pewter and tin demonstrations. Craftsmen and craftswomen, toiling daily in the village since its 1929 dedication, produced thousands of beautifully hand-shaped items during the ensuing 50 years and, at the same time, provided fascinating educational experiences for millions of visitors (24, 25 and 26).

23

24

25

26

Activity was just as fervent in and around the museum. A Lovett Hall area once occupied by squash courts consolidated the holdings of the Robert Hudson Tannahill Research Library. New professional offices replaced laboratories and classrooms.

In the museum itself, the Garden Room Restaurant, originally a high school laboratory, was replaced with a museum book and souvenir shop. Covered-over courtyards enclosed folk art and musical instrument galleries. To take the place of the old cafeteria, a large, two-story addition, Heritage Hall, was added to the east end of the building, providing cafeteria service downstairs and sit-down service upstairs.

While all these improvements sought to enhance the experience of visitors, traditional and new special events encouraged more overt involvement. Historical vignettes, outdoor dramas (27), roving musical groups and a Town Hall variety show kicked off the Old Time Summer Festival in 1971. The summer-long village entertainment program developed into an annual event.

The Autumn Harvest Festival and Antique Fire Apparatus Muster debuted in 1972. In 1973 the Colonial Military Muster marched into the village (28). An Ancient Fife & Drum Corps Muster in 1978 showed the lighter side of military life.

28

29

30

31

32

The village remained a popular setting for live media broadcasts, including a week's telecast of the "Phil Donahue Show" in 1973 (29, with Gladys Knight and the Pips in Town Hall), and two local radio shows: J. P. McCarthy's "Focus," also in 1973 (30, with institute chief conservator Edward Gilbert, left), and the "Jimmy Launce Show."

Special programs attempted to interest visitors in village and museum resources during the evening and off-season weekends. The evening events—Evening in the Park, Village Winter Evening, Museum Evening to Remember—usually included a meal and compact tour. Craft and cooking demonstrations began on fall weekends in 1977 (31). Dinner-theater packages enhanced several different plays put on by the Greenfield Village Players each year (32, Under the Gaslight).

163

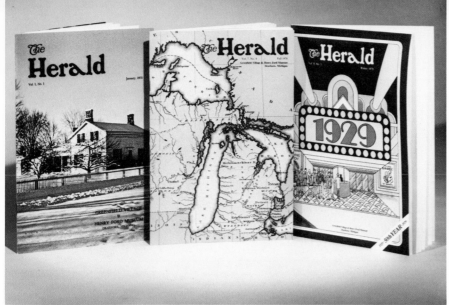

35

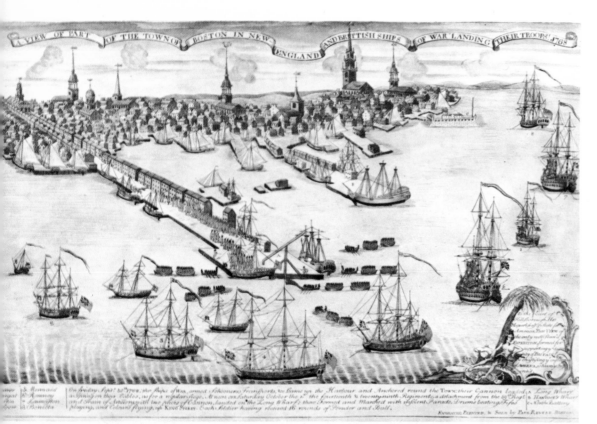

Formed in 1971, the Friends of Greenfield Village and Henry Ford Museum provide vital support to Edison Institute programs. Individual, family and corporate members contribute yearly to the operation and special activities of the complex. Significant donations over the years made possible the acquisition of a c. 1765 portrait of Mrs. John Duncan by Thomas McIlworth, Schenectady, New York (33). This painting was thus reunited with its mate, McIlworth's portrait of Mr. John Duncan (c. 1765), which the museum already owned.

The Friends also presented to the museum a colored engraving by Paul Revere: A View of Part of the Town of Boston in New England and Brittish (sic) Ships of War Landing Their Troops! 1768 (34). Designed and colored by Christian Remick, the print is one of Revere's largest, rarest and most interesting works.

In turn, the more than 9,000 "Friends" participate in outings, attend special exhibition previews and receive numerous benefits, such as giftshop discounts, free admission and the quarterly Herald magazine (35), which delves into museum collections and the American past.

36

Continuing the exhibit traditions of earlier years, between 1970 and 1979 the staff produced a number of significant portrayals of American life, including: "Colonial Agriculture Exhibit," 1975; "100 Years of the Phonograph," 1977 (36); and "Pittsburgh Glass," 1977.

The Bicentennial year, 1976, featured several special displays. "Warp and Weft," a hands-on exhibit of early textile production (37), returned for its second year and became an annual event. Two other shows focused on "Great Americans" and "Centennial Memories" (38, in the new Folk Art Gallery).

37

38

41

40

The major exhibit during the year and probably of the decade was "The Struggle and The Glory." Based on hundreds of previously unpublished manuscripts, letters and other Revolutionary era documents from the museum's Bicentennial collection (39, 1823 facsimile of the Declaration of Independence), and supported by original artifacts, the exhibit traced America's efforts to wrench herself free of British rule. Numerous staff members worked long hours preparing the huge exhibit areas (40, Crafts and Presentation Director Douglas Hough at left), but the effort paid off when the visiting public learned about the nation's beginning and the various people participating in that birth (41, young visitors viewing George Washington's camp chest).

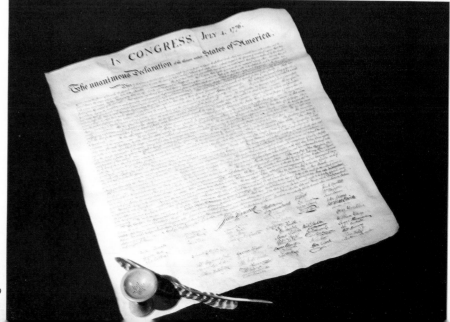

39

A Golden Year

The dawning of 1979, the institute's 50th anniversary, saw its staff determined to include as many people as possible in the celebration. Respecting Henry Ford's educational ideals, the planning of events stressed the relationship of the past to the present.

Fifty-year observances began in 1978 with the rededication of the museum cornerstone and the activation of the machinery in Edison's Fort Myers Laboratory. Special anniversary tours of the museum and village in the winter months of 1979 emphasized: the development of lighting; Edison's other inventions and their impact on daily life; and some of Henry Ford's lesser-known activities and interests. A commemorative exhibit in the village's Menlo Park Compound opened on Edison's birthday, February 11. And, from February through May, the Famous Americans Lecture Series featured addresses on Thomas Edison, George Washington Carver, Charles F. Kettering and Henry Ford.

Other planned activities included: the reenactment of the October 1929 ceremonies (drawing world-wide attention as the official recognition of the 100th anniversary of electric light); the reactivation of the Menlo Park Machine Shop; the cataloging of Edison archival material within the institute; a reunion of village school alumni and teachers; the inauguration on April 11 (Henry and Clara Ford's wedding anniversary) of an annual Founders' Day commemoration; special museum exhibits; an anniversary play in Town Hall; and, on the last day of the year, a special train ride and relighting of the Menlo Park complex. For it was on New Year's Eve, 1879, that Edison lighted several Menlo Park buildings and adjacent streets to demonstrate to the press and public that his lighting system worked in practice as well as in the laboratory.

GOLDEN JUBILEE

1929   1979

HENRY   THOMAS
FORD   EDISON

THE EDISON INSTITUTE

42

43

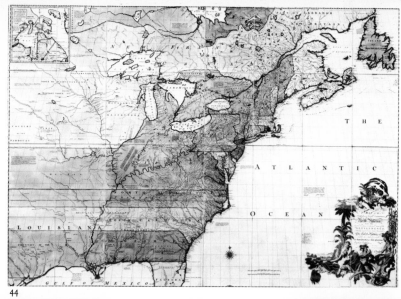

44

45

Even while engaged in extensive development projects, the curatorial staff continued to refine the collections. The more significant acquisitions included: a 1740 Queen Anne linen press (42), a gift of Mrs. Eleanor Clay Ford; the Shaker textile collection (43), representing several 19th-century Shaker communities in New England and the Midwest; and a map of British and French dominions in North America (44), drawn by John Mitchell c. 1755.

Two other new collection items joined the transportation area. North Central Airlines presented the museum with a 1939 DC-3 aircraft (45). The plane, which had more passenger flight hours logged than any other existing aircraft, landed at the Ford Test Track (the former Ford Airport) in 1975 and required partial disassembly and hoisting over a fence before it "landed" in its exhibit area at the rear of the museum. In addition to the DC-3, a 1929 Packard custom-built roadster (46) found a home in the museum. One of 50 produced and the only one still known to exist, the car had retailed for $5,260 in the fall of 1928.

46

Though the village schools closed in 1969, The Edison Institute's educational programs grew steadily throughout the 1970s to include students of all ages and interests. Children spending "A Day in a One Room School," inaugurated in the Miller School in 1972 (47), enjoyed the program so much that the institute opened the McGuffey School for the same purpose in 1976 (48). Once again, children could learn from McGuffey's Readers and study the historic objects around them, as Henry Ford had believed in so strongly. The institute offered a flourishing day and evening adult education curriculum (49, chair caning) and initiated special internships for students pursuing a degree in museum-practice programs. At the first annual Educators' Day in 1978, teachers personally viewed the wealth of learning experiences available to their students during field trips and overnight visits, or, with institute educational materials and publications, right in their own classrooms.

Near the conclusion of the village development program, the institute added its first historic structure in 15 years when Mrs. C. McGregory Wells donated an 18th-century Connecticut saltbox house and its colonial furnishings. After crews painstakingly dismantled and trucked the house to Dearborn in 1977, they reconstructed it at the end of South Dearborn Road between the Cape Cod Windmill and the Cotswold Forge in 1978.

53

50

51

The saltbox house was accustomed to moving. Mrs. Wells found the Andover, Connecticut, dwelling in 1951 (50) and had it disassembled and moved 35 miles to Union, Connecticut. Once restored in its new location, the house served as Mrs. Wells' home for the next 26 years. Following her donation of the house to Greenfield Village and its 1977 disassembly (51), restoration specialists George Watson and Donald Graham watched carefully as workers unloaded numbered pieces (52), poured the foundation and, shortly thereafter, began careful reconstruction (53). In the early summer of 1978, the house was ready to receive its first village visitors (54). The public continues to find the saltbox house a fascinating flashback to New England's pioneering past (55, kitchen and 56, parlor).

Although other old buildings will undoubtedly augment Henry Ford's Greenfield Village in future years, the scene in 1979 represented a community teeming with life as lived by earlier generations of Americans.

52

54

56

55

Technology Explained

The goal of effectively communicating to the public the story of America's technological progress inspired the reinstallation of museum displays. The concept for the new Hall of Technology (which includes exhibits on transportation, lighting and communications, power and shop machinery, home arts, firearms and agriculture, as well as the Street of Early American Shops and the Interpretive Center) relied on selective presentation. Rather than displaying numerous examples of the same general type of artifact and letting the visitor determine the interrelationships, curators chose one artifact to represent several. That one object and its use are now fully explained to the visitor.

In the transportation area, for example, the museum's collection now means more than simply an impressive number of vehicles. A comprehensive story line explains to visitors the development of transportation in America.

Curators had to justify the inclusion of each and every object in their exhibit on the basis of its contribution to the overall story. They removed from exhibit those artifacts not meeting that criterion and grouped them into study collections. Those items remaining on display represent the best Americans could produce *at the time* for the use intended. Exhibited objects illustrate either significant inventions or refinements of existing technology that tell the story of American industrial growth.

The removal of duplicate objects also provided room for more useful and instructive display techniques. Visitors can identify each major collection within the hall by the color used in the signs and carpeting. The red transportation carpeting, for example, visually highlights the dark tones of many early automobiles. Vehicles no longer crowd each other in seemingly endless rows, but stand in logical groupings. More space around each car allows viewing from several angles as well as glimpses of interiors and engine compartments.

Almost as important as the artifacts in communicating America's heritage are the labels that explain them. For the first few years after the museum opened five decades ago, perhaps 80 percent of the visitors could recognize and identify all exhibited objects (with the probable exception of the Edisoniana and electronics artifacts) from personal experience. They could enjoy displays without the aid of labels. Probably no more than 5 percent of today's visitors can readily identify the objects. Thus, each year labels grow more vital to the effectiveness of the exhibits.

By examining existing labels and visitor needs, the museum staff determined three educational requirements for the new labels: to identify the object; to relate it to similar objects; and to place the object in the context of society. This last goal prompted the creation of an Interpretive Center or introductory "museum." The 30,000-square-foot center, with key items from each major collection, constituted the last step in the Hall of Technology redesign project. Here, after experiencing the comprehensive story of American technological progress, visitors can move out into the separate collection areas that most interest them.

To fulfill the second goal, introductory boards explain general groupings at key points in each collection area. Finally, each object possesses an accurate, informative label of its own. Today's visitor has become accustomed, through radio and television, to receiving messages in succinct doses. The new label system accomplishes rapid transmittal of information through the various label levels. The visitor can become as involved as he or she wishes, going no further than the introductory boards, reading one or two sentences on an object label or requesting more detailed information and access to study collections from curators. The system attempts to provide people with as much information as they want without overwhelming them.

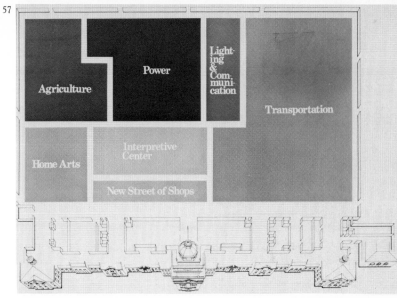

57

Comparing the eight-acre Hall of Technology's new layout with that of the mid-1950s on page 147 illustrates the enormous change in the presentation of artifacts (57, overall view and 58, detail of transportation section). Regardless of size, artifacts were moved to dramatize more effectively the story of America's technological progress (59, Sikorsky helicopter).

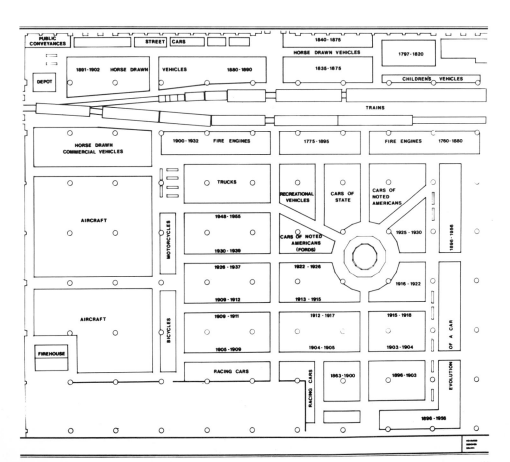

58

59

The new Interpretive Center, or mini-museum, features time capsules displaying artifacts from a given time period grouped together to illustrate life-styles in that era. Other areas of the center explain the various collections located throughout the Hall of Technology. By mid-April of 1979, workmen had completed the exterior of a second Street of Shops (60) and the museum staff was concentrating on the Interpretive Center (61, arranging graphics) for the June 1 opening (62). The camera recorded the transformation of Hall of Technology collection areas from the old to the new (63, agricultural exhibit "before" and 64, "after"; 65, former chronological row approach in the transportation area and 66, present thematic groupings).

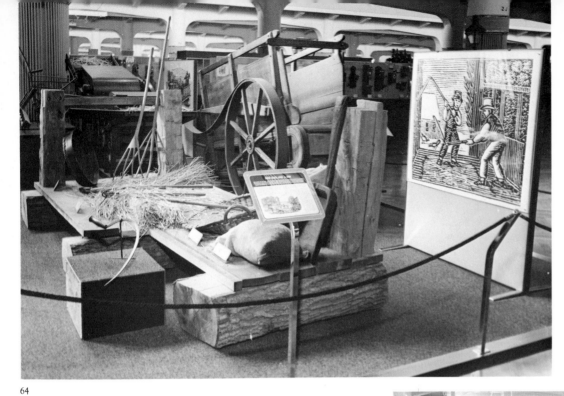

64

65

63

66

Appendix C

Attendance Milestones

Pre-opening attendance	October 1929 to June 1933	28,170
First full year of operation	1934	243,295
First year to exceed 500,000	1937	547,621
Pre-war peak	1940	633,296
First year to exceed 1 million	1960	1,006,664
First year to exceed 1.5 million	1971	1,547,589
All-time high attendance	1976	1,751,126
All-time low attendance	1943	126,036
One-day attendance record	Old Car Festival, 1972	24,262
10 millionth visitor	1955	
20 millionth visitor	1964	
25 millionth visitor	1968	
40 millionth visitor	1978	

Appendix D

Edison Institute General Information

ADDRESS

20900 Oakwood Boulevard, Dearborn, Michigan 48121, (313)271-1620

ACCREDITATION

1976 by the American Association of Museums

Greenfield Village and Henry Ford Museum are incorporated as The Edison Institute, a Michigan non-profit, indoor/outdoor, educational institution which is independent of both the Ford Foundation and the Ford Motor Company. Both museum facilities are open year-round except on Thanksgiving, Christmas and New Year's days.

EMPLOYEES

340 full-time and 850 part-time (at peak operating schedule)

ACREAGE

260 acres, 14 of which are occupied by Henry Ford Museum

NUMBER OF GREENFIELD VILLAGE BUILDINGS

107 historic and associated buildings
  4 support structures: Lovett Hall,
    radio shack, gatehouse and
    souvenir shop
  3 food facilities

114 TOTAL

Acknowledgments

The author wishes to acknowledge the invaluable assistance of The Edison Institute management and staff in the research, preparation and production of this history, which is so meaningful to us all. Special thanks go to the men and women working in the Ford Archives, Publications and Photographic departments, whose assorted talents made this work possible.

Personal gratitude is extended to those listed below and especially to Sarah Lawrence of the Ford Archives for her unflagging and inspired photographic and general research; Monica Valant, editorial secretary, for her encouragement and efficiency; Doug Bakken, director of the Ford Archives and Tannahill Research Library, for his leadership and support; Don Ross, free-lance designer, for his talent and dedication; and my wife, Meredith, for her patience and critical eye.

Manuscript Editors
Lois Livesay, *Publications department*
Susan Flierl, *Publications department*

Research Assistance
Dave Glick, *Education department*
Win Sears, *Ford Archives*
Joan VanVlerah, *Ford Archives*
Marion White, *Education department*
Eileen Griffin, *Education department*

Photographic Services
Carl Malotka, *Photographic department*
Rudy Ruzicska, *Photographic department*
Al Harvey, *Photographic department*
Tim Hunter, *Photographic department*

Index